A
World Guide to
Whales,
Dolphins,
and Porpoises

67284

Other books by Donald S. Heintzelman

The Hawks of New Jersey
A Guide to Northeastern Hawk Watching
Finding Birds in Trinidad and Tobago
Autumn Hawk Flights
A Guide to Eastern Hawk Watching
North American Ducks, Geese & Swans
Hawks and Owls of North America
A Guide to Hawk Watching in North America
A Manual for Bird Watching in the Americas
The Illustrated Bird Watcher's Dictionary

A World Guide to Whales, Dolphins, and Porpoises

Donald S. Heintzelman

Paintings by
Rod Arbogast

Winchester Press
Tulsa, Oklahoma

Copyright© 1981 by Donald S. Heintzelman
All rights reserved

Library of Congress Cataloging in Publication Data

Heintzelman, Donald S.
  A world guide to whales, dolphins, and porpoises.

  Bibliography: p. 143
  Includes index.
  1. Cetacea—Identification. I. Arbogast, Rod.
II. Title.
QL737.C4H35   599.5   80-20823
ISBN 0-87691-323-0

Published by Winchester Press
P. O. Box 1260
1421 South Sheridan
Tulsa, Oklahoma 74101

Book Design by Janice L. Merz

Printed in the United States of America

1 2 3 4 5   85 84 83 82 81

Cover Photo
© *Betsy Blass, National Audubon Society Collection/Photo Researchers.*

To Carol,
who cares about whales
and all creatures large and small.

——CONTENTS——

ARTIST'S PLATES

MAPS

——— PREFACE ———

My interest in whales, dolphins, and porpoises began in 1974 in the equatorial Pacific Ocean as I sailed from mainland Ecuador to the Galapagos Islands. I remember vividly watching dolphins pacing the ship by tropical moonlight. Later that year I again watched dolphins in the equatorial north Atlantic Ocean off South America from the decks of the M. S. *Lindblad Explorer* on which I served as ornithologist. In the weeks following, I also watched delightful Amazon River Dolphins as we sailed up the Amazon and explored numerous feeder tributaries to that great waterway.

In later Amazon voyages, *Inia* was seen frequently. At times the similar Tucuxi Dolphin also was noted. A year later, aboard the *Lindblad Explorer* again in the south Atlantic Ocean off South America, a splendid Sperm Whale appeared just off our port side. Everybody on the bridge, including the Captain, ran to the port wing and looked down upon the gigantic creature.

On December 10, 1975, I again stood on deck on the *Lindblad Explorer* as we sailed along the South Georgia coastline, then into beautiful Cumberland Bay, and docked at the abandoned whaling station, Grytviken. Thousands of whales were slaughtered there three-quarters of a century earlier. At times the water ran red with the blood of the unfortunate creatures. Now, not a whale was in sight. Only white bones of whales long dead littered the bay shoreline. Nearby, rusting hulks of old whale chasers and equally rusting tools and machinery reminded us of the miserable activities that once occurred there.

Later, at other abandoned Antarctic whaling stations on Deception Island and at Port Lockroy, more bones and remnants from the whale slaughter days were seen. But the whales were gone. During weeks of sailing through Antarctic waters once famous as prime whaling grounds, less than a handful of whales appeared.

Still, whaling continues. This slaughter has caused worldwide alarm and action on the part of concerned conservationists—often laymen rather than scientists—who deplore the slaughter of these gentle, gigantic, intelligent animals of the oceans. Russia and Japan are particularly active despite the strong voices of world opinion aimed against them. The net result is that fewer and fewer whales survive. But some do.

This guide, therefore, is designed to provide sailors, mariners, sea voyagers, bird and whale watchers, and other persons who venture onto the oceans and seas of the world with illustrations and basic species information which will help them to recognize and identify most of the species of whales, dolphins, and porpoises they see. For a variety of reasons, that task frequently is very difficult. Indeed, many species of cetaceans are poorly known, even to scientists. Not infrequently scientists do not even agree on the number of existing species. Probably new species still await discovery. Others, now considered full species, may yet be reduced to subspecific status as new and more complete information becomes available. Meanwhile, confusion rages in the scientific cetacean literature. The situation is unavoidable at this stage in our knowledge of these marine mammals. Nevertheless, conservationists can't wait until all the academic problems are resolved before acting. This guide, therefore, is designed also to fill an existing gap and provide conservationists and scientists with a useful tool to help them in their battle to save these splendid creatures.

A variety of books were consulted during the preparation of this guide, including Burton's *The Life and Death of Whales,* Coffey's *Dolphins, Whales and Porpoises,* Daugherty's *Marine Mammals of California,* Hall and Kelson's *The Mammals of North America,* Hershkovitz's *Catalog of Living Whales,* Katona, Richardson, and Hazard's *A Field Guide to the Whales and Seals of the Gulf of Maine,* Kraus and Katona's *Humpback Whales (Megaptera novaeanglinae) in the North Atlantic–A Catalog of Identified Individuals,* Leatherwood, Caldwell, and Winn's *Whales, Dolphins, and Porpoises of the Western North Atlantic–A Guide to Their Identification,* Leatherwood, Evans, and Rice's *The Whales, Dolphins, and Porpoises of the Eastern North Pacific–A Guide to Their Identification in the Water,* Lockley's *Whales, Dolphins and Porpoises,* Matthews' *The Whale* and *Penguins, Whalers, and Sealers,* McIntyre's *Mind in the Waters,* Miller's *The World of the California Gray Whale,* Miller and Kellogg's *List of North American Recent Mammals,* Mörzer Bruyns' *Field Guide of Whales and Dolphins,* Murphy's *Logbook for Grace* and *A Dead Whale or a Stove Boat,* Rice's *A List of the Marine Mammals of the World,* Scheffer's *A Natural History of Marine Mammals,* Walker's *Whale Primer,* and Winn and Olla's *Behavior of Marine Animals* (Volume 3, cetaceans).

Additional reference was made to cetacean information published in various periodicals including *Alaska Geographic, Angeles*

Gate, Atlantic Naturalist, Audubon, Defenders, Living Wilderness, Maclean's Magazine, National Geographic, Nature Society News, New Jersey Audubon, and *Noticias de Galapagos.*

The following agencies, organizations, and companies provided helpful information used in the preparation of this book: Allied Whale, Bermuda Department of Agriculture and Fisheries, Cabrillo Marine Museum, Cabrillo National Monument, California Department of Parks and Recreation, Capitol Records, College of the Atlantic, Folkways Records, General Whale, Glacier Bay National Monument, International Whaling Commission, Lahaina Restoration Foundation, Los Angeles Recreation and Park Department, Maine Bureau of Parks and Recreation, National Marine Mammal Laboratory, Pacific Rim National Park (Canada), Point Reyes National Seashore, Redwood Empire Association, Sea World, The Whale Center, Whale Protection Fund, and World Wildlife Fund. Additional information and services were provided by the Allentown Public Library, Muhlenberg College Library, and the office of Congressman Donald Ritter.

Information contained in the appendix on federal laws is adapted from a circular entitled "The Humpback Whale," distributed by the Lahaina Restoration Foundation. Sample whale sighting report forms used in the appendix were provided by Allied Whale, Cabrillo Marine Museum, and the National Oceanic and Atmospheric Administration.

The following persons also provided assistance or information during the preparation of this book: Ruth C. Adams, Andrew J. Berger, Carl W. Buchheister, John F. Chapman, Helen G. Cruickshank, Ray Gambell, Theodore R. Hake, Thomas Johnson, Steven K. Katona, Steve King, John H. Knight, Scott Kraus, James C. Luckey, John M. Olguin, William F. Marshall, Maxine McCloskey, Mark Nyhof, Joel and Linda Pretz, Mary M. Reynolds, William and Mia Rossiter, Richard A. Rowlett, John L. Sansing, Leighton Taylor, Michael F. Tillman, Thomas R. Tucker, Frederick A. Ulmer, and David B. Wingate.

Photographs used in this book were provided by the following agencies, institutions, and organizations: Cabrillo National Monument, Los Angeles Recreation and Park Department, National Marine Mammal Laboratory, Oregon State University Sea Grant College Program, and Sea World. Additional photographs were provided by the following persons: Alan Brady, Jeffrey Goodyear, Steven Katona, Scott Kraus, James R. Larison, Geoffrey Ohland,

William and Mia Rossiter, and Mark Towner. A few of my own photographs are used as well.

Rod Arbogast painted the artist's plates especially for use in this book.

I would like to express my appreciation to each of the agencies, institutions, organizations, companies, and persons who assisted in one way or another in this conservation-education effort on behalf of the world's cetaceans.

Allentown, Pa.   Donald S. Heintzelman
7 March 1980

CHECKLIST
OF WHALES

( )   Alula Whale

( )   Atlantic Pilot Whale

( )   Baird's Beaked Whale

( )   Black Right Whale

( )   Blainville's Beaked Whale

( )   Blue Whale

( )   Bowdoini's Beaked Whale

( )   Bowhead Whale

( )   Bryde's Whale

( )   Camperdown Whale

( )   Cuvier's Beaked Whale

( )   Dwarf Sperm Whale

( )   False Killer Whale

( )   Fin Whale

( )   Gray Whale

( )   Gulf Stream Beaked Whale

( )   Hector's Beaked Whale

( )   Hubb's Beaked Whale

( )   Humpback Whale

( )   Japanese Beaked Whale

( )   Killer Whale

( )   Little Killer Whale

( )   Minke Whale

( )   Narwhal

( )   North Sea Beaked Whale

( )   Northern Bottlenose Whale

CHECKLIST OF DOLPHINS

( )   Amazon River Dolphin

( )   Atlantic Spotted Dolphin

( )   Atlantic White-Sided Dolphin

( )   Blackchin Dolphin

( )   Blue Dolphin

( )   Bottlenosed Dolphin

( )   Bridled Dolphin

( )   Cameroon Dolphin

( )   Chinese Lake Dolphin

( )   Chinese White Dolphin

( )   Commerson's Dolphin

( )   Common Dolphin

( )   Dusky Dolphin

( )   Ganges Dolphin

( )   Guiana River Dolphin

( )   Heaviside's Dolphin

( )   Hector's Dolphin

( )   Hourglass Dolphin

( )   Irrawaddy River Dolphin

( )   La Plata Dolphin

( )   Long-Beaked Dolphin

( )   Narrow-Snouted Dolphin

( )   Northern Right Whale Dolphin

( )   Pacific White-Sided Dolphin

( )   Plumbeous Dolphin

( )   Rio de Janeiro Dolphin

CHECKLIST OF PORPOISES

( )   Black Finless Porpoise

( )   Black Porpoise

( )   Dall's Porpoise

( )   Gulf of California Porpoise

( )   Harbor Porpoise

( )   Spectacled Porpoise

1
SPECIES ACCOUNTS

Balaenopteridae: Rorqual Whales

The rorqual whales are distinguished by a series of grooves on their throats and torpedo-shaped heads. In addition, their dorsal fins are distinct. Unlike other whales with baleens, those of the rorquals are shorter and more numerous.

Minke Whale *Balaenoptera acutorostrata*   Plate 2

Other Names: Piked Whale, Lesser Rorqual, Little Piked Whale.
Length: 30 feet (9 meters).
Weight: 20,000 pounds (9,072 kilograms).
Description: The smallest of the rorqual whales. Grayish above, large light-gray areas on the sides of the body, and lighter grayish-white below with a prominent white flipper patch (often lacking in southern hemisphere specimens) and yellow-white baleen plates. There also is a prominent dorsal fin. The spout can reach up to six feet (1.8 meters). Generally, only one or two individuals are seen when the species is reported.
Food: Fish, krill, and squid (rarely).
Habitat: Coastal waters. Occasionally marine and oceanic waters.
Distribution: In the north Atlantic and Arctic Oceans from Spitzbergen south to the Mediterranean and Black Seas on the eastern side, and Baffin Bay south to Florida on the western side; in the south Atlantic Ocean from Rio de La Plata, Argentina, and Cape of Good Hope south to the ice shelf of the Ant-

Minke Whale's pale side patches visible (photo by William Rossiter).

arctic; in the north Pacific Ocean from the Bering Sea south to
Baja California, and from Siberia south to the Sea of Japan and
the Yellow Sea; in the south Pacific Ocean from Chile,
Australia, and New Zealand to latitude 78⁰ south and the Antarctic ice shelf; in the Indian Ocean from South Africa to Java
and the Bay of Bengal.

Sei Whale *Balaenoptera borealis*   Plate 1

Other Names: None.
Length: 58 feet (17.4 meters).
Weight: Up to 46,000 pounds (20,865 kilograms).
Description: Variable in color but often dark gray above and spotted
on the sides, but whitish on the throat, chest, and belly with
relatively short ventral grooves which terminate in front of the
navel. The baleen plates are a distinctive grayish white and
have a fine, soft texture on their inner edges. There is a rather
large prominent dorsal fin. The spout can rise up to 14 feet
(4.2 meters). At a distance, it can be confused with the
Fin Whale.
Food: Small fish, squid, krill.
Habitat: Coastal and marine waters.
Distribution: In all the seas. In the north Atlantic and Arctic Oceans
from Spitzbergen south to Spain and North Africa (Cap Blanc)
on the eastern side, and from the Davis Strait and Labrador
south to Campeche, Mexico, on the western side; in the south
Atlantic Ocean from Angola and South Africa and coastal
Brazil (20° S.) south to the Antarctic (65° S.); in the north

Pacific Ocean from Siberia south to Korea and Japan in the western portion, and from western Alaska south to Baja California in the eastern portion; in the south Pacific Ocean in waters around Australia, New Zealand, and Borneo, and from Ecuador and Galapagos south to Chile; also in Indonesian waters in the Indian Ocean.

Bryde's Whale *Balaenoptera edeni*   Plate 2

Other Name: Bryden's Whale.
Length: 50 feet (15 meters).
Weight: 36,000 pounds (16,330 kilograms).
Description: Very similar to the Sei Whale but with three longitudinal ridges on the top of the head, a dark chin, throat and chest (white in Sei Whale), the ventral grooves extending back as far as the navel; also stiffer, longer, and much thicker fingers on the baleen plate. The species has a smaller and perhaps more triangular dorsal fin than the Sei Whale.
Food: Gregarious fish such as mackerel and herring.
Habitat: Coastal and marine waters.
Distribution: In the Indian Ocean from South Africa to Australia; in the Atlantic Ocean from Norway southward to Senegal and the Cape of Good Hope and the West Indies (Grenada and Curacao); in the Pacific Ocean known to occur in waters around Baja California in the eastern portion and waters around Japan in the west; also the Barin Islands and New Zealand.

Blue Whale *Balaenoptera musculus*   Plate 1

Other Name: Sulphur-Bottom Whale.
Length: 110 feet (33 meters).
Weight: 300,000 pounds (136,000 kilograms).
Description: Enormous. Slate blue above mottled with white spots on the back and upper sides; broad and U-shaped head only about one-quarter the total body length. Dorsal fin unusually small, triangular, and located far back on the body, and the grooves on the underside extending back about a third of the body length. Blue Whales are the largest animals ever to appear on the earth. Individuals from the southern oceans are larger than those of the northern oceans. Generally reported alone or in pairs. Can be confused with the Fin Whale at a distance.

Food: Krill (consumed in enormous quantities).

Habitat: Deep waters in polar and oceanic areas and sometimes in shallow inshore waters.

Distribution: Most common north of 35° north latitude in the Atlantic, Pacific, Arctic, and Indian Oceans and south to pack ice from 40° south latitude; also from waters off Rio Grande do Sul, Brazil, and Ecuador south to the ice. There are additional records from Hawaii and northern Panama.

Fin Whale   *Balaenoptera physalus*   Plate 1

Other Names: Finback, Common Rorqual, Razorback.

Length: 81 feet (24.3 meters).

Weight: 128,000 pounds (58,000 kilograms).

Description: Second in size only to the Blue Whale but with a more slender body and the head narrower and more V-shaped than the Blue Whale. Pale gray above, white below, with well-marked ventral grooves. The dorsal fin is taller and more back-curved than in the Blue Whale. The flippers and flukes are white on their undersurface. The color of the baleen plates is distinctive by being asymmetrical—grayish-blue except for yellow-white on the front right side. The color of the outside of the lower jaw also is asymmetrical—white on the right side but blue-gray (pigmented) on the left side. Individuals from the southern hemisphere are larger than those from the northern hemisphere. The spout can reach 20 feet (6 meters) in height. May be confused with the Blue Whale and the Sei Whale. Fin Whales often travel in groups of 6 or 7 individuals.

Food: Krill and small fish.

Habitat: Deep waters which, in summer, are outside of the polar pack ice.

Distribution: From equatorial waters northward to the pack ice in the Indian, Pacific, and Atlantic Oceans; also from Caribbean Panama south to the Falkland Islands and Tierra del Fuego in the Atlantic Ocean, and from Ecuadorian Pacific Ocean waters south to the pack ice at about 75° south latitude.

Humpback Whale   *Megaptera novaeangliae*   Plates 2 and 3

Other Names: Hump Whale, Humpbacked Whale, Hunchbacked Whale, Bunch.

Length: 53 feet (16.2 meters).

Fin Whale's back and dorsal fin (photo by William Rossiter).

Fin Whale feeding; ventral
grooves on belly visible (photo by Geoffrey Ohland).

Fin Whale's rostrum and white lower-right jaw (photo by Jeffrey Goodyear).

Humpback Whale's back and dorsal fin; side of head.
(photo by Mark Towner, National Marine Mammal Laboratory).

Humpback Whale's flukes (photo by Steven Katona).

Weight: 90,000 pounds (40,824 kilograms).

Description: Variable in color but markedly different from the other rorqual whales. Stocky or chunky. Black on top (blue-gray or blue in the other species) shading to white on the throat and undersides. A variety of protuberances and knobs mark the head and flippers. Not infrequently the animal is covered with barnacles and whale lice. The small dorsal fin varies in shape and is located in the middle of the back. The flippers are distinctive by being unusually long and narrow, often a third the length of the whale, with the edges being irregular. The relatively few ventral grooves extend back to the umbilicus. The back edge of the flukes is scalloped, and the coloration patterns of the undersides of the flukes vary from almost completely white to almost all black; each Humpback Whale has its own unique fluke pattern, however, thus allowing for positive recognition of specific individuals. Humpbacks frequently make spectacular breaches out of the water followed by splashes which are visible at great distances. The spout can reach heights of 12 feet (3.6 meters). The species has extraordinarily beautiful, haunting songs which sometimes last for several hours. The animals are known to change their songs yearly.

Food: Krill and smaller fish in schools.

Habitat: Deep coastal waters and banks, but sometimes visible from coastal dunes, headlands, and cliffs.

Distribution: From the Antarctic to the Arctic in all the seas. In the north Atlantic Ocean from Puerto Rico northward at least to Greenland, and in the north Pacific Ocean from Mexico northward along the North American coast to Alaska and the Bering Sea. Off eastern South America from Venezuela south past Cape Horn, and off western South America from southern Panama south past Cape Horn to 68° south latitude. The waters off Bermuda, the Hawaiian Islands, and certain other areas are among the major calving grounds. Distinctive populations occur in the north Atlantic, north Pacific, and southern hemisphere oceans.

Balaenidae: **Right Whales**

The right whales (so called because the early whalers considered them the right whales to capture) *lack a dorsal fin* and ventral grooves. They have several hundred long, narrow baleen (whalebone) plates on each side of the mouth. Their spout produces a double jet.

Bowhead Whale *Balaena mysticetus*   Plate 4

Other Names: Greenland Right Whale, Bowhead, Arctic Right
    Whale, Ice Whale, Great Polar Whale.
Length: 65 feet (19.8 meters).
Weight: 244,000 pounds (110,678 kilograms).
Description: A splendid chunky whale whose enormous head forms
    one-third of the entire length of the animal. It is mostly dark
    black or bluish-gray, but the throat is pale or whitish and there
    may be a wide, conspicuous grayish or whitish band just an-
    terior to the flukes. The eyes are located on each side of the
    body just behind the corners of the mouth and above the flip-
    pers. The mouth is gigantic and each side contains more than
    350 black baleen plates each almost 14 feet (4 meters) long.
    The two blowholes are placed on the top of the head about
    midway back. There is no dorsal fin. The spout is V-shaped
    and rises from 10 to 13 feet (3 to 3.9 meters) into the air.
Food: Krill.
Habitat: Within or close to the Arctic pack ice.
Distribution: The Arctic Ocean southward in the north Atlantic to
    the Gulf of St. Lawrence (rare off the Massachusetts coast); al-
    so southward to the Bering, Okhotsk, and Barents Seas. Form-
    erly reported in the north Pacific Ocean to the Sea of Japan.

Black Right Whale *Eubalaena glacialis*   Plate 4

Other Names: Right Whale, Southern Right Whale, Biscay Right
    Whale.
Length: 53 feet (16.2 meters).
Weight: 144,000 pounds (65,319 kilograms).
Description: A rotund whale without a dorsal fin or ridge. The body
    is mottled brown (occasionally black) on the back whereas the
    chin and belly are white. Sometimes grayish-white scars are
    present. The long, narrow upper jaw is highly arched as are
    the lips. There are distinctive, whitish, horny-like crusty
    growths called the bonnet on the top of the upper jaw. The
    large mouth forms about one-sixth the length of the animal and
    contains several hundred very long, narrow, dark brown to
    black baleen plates on each side. The flippers are fairly large.

Black Right Whale (photo by Geoffrey Ohland).

The V-shaped (double) spout angles forward into plumes up to 16 feet (4.8 meters) high. The species can be confused with Gray Whales (in the Pacific Ocean) at a distance.

Food: Plankton (mostly copepods).

Habitat: Coastal and marine waters, frequently close to islands.

Distribution: The world's temperate and polar oceans. There are separate subspecies in the north Atlantic, north Pacific, and southern hemisphere. The north Atlantic race (*E. g. glacialis*) ranges on the eastern side from Spitzbergen and Iceland south to the Mediterranean, and on the western side from the Davis Strait south to Bermuda and the Gulf of Mexico; the north Pacific race (*E. g. japonica*) ranges from 20 degrees north southward to the Sea of Okhotsk, the Bering Sea, and the Gulf of Alaska; the southern hemisphere race (*E. g. australis*) ranges from 13° to 20° south to 65° south in the south Atlantic, south Pacific, and Indian Oceans.

Pygmy Right Whale *Caperea marginata*   Plate 4

Other Names: None.

Length: 20 feet (6 meters).

Weight: 10,000 pounds (4,536 kilograms).

Description: A rare, little-known black whale sometimes showing a whitish belly. The white baleen plates are marked with a black or dark brown outer edge. The small dorsal fin is sickle-shaped. The flippers are positioned unusually far back on the sides of the body.

Food: Krill.

Habitat: Marine and oceanic waters.

Distribution: The waters of the southern hemisphere. In the south

Atlantic Ocean from the vicinity of Buenos Aires, Argentina, southward past the Falkland Islands to Cape Horn and South Africa; in the south Pacific Ocean chiefly the waters around New Zealand and Australia; in the Indian Ocean along the southwestern and southern Australian coasts.

Gray Whale's flukes in dive (photo by William Rossiter).

Eschrichtidae: Gray Whales

The single species in this family lacks a dorsal fin but replaces it with a series of small humps on the posterior portion of the back. In addition, the two to four grooves on the throat are poorly defined. There are only 150 baleen plates on each side of the jaw. Females are somewhat larger than males.

Gray Whale *Eschrichtius (robustus) gibbosus*   Plate 5

Other Names: California Gray Whale, Mossback, Devilfish.
Length: 45 feet (13.5 meters).
Weight: 40,000 pounds (18,144 kilograms).
Description: A dark brown-gray whale with numerous white blotch-
    es and spots (barnacles and scars) on the body and head. No
    dorsal fin. The 150 pale yellow baleen plates are short and
    thick, and the throat grooves are minimal in definition. There
    are tactile bristles on the jaws and on the two blowholes. The

spout erupts into a V-shape and reaches heights up to about 10 feet (3 meters).

Food: Copepods, sea cucumbers, and small fish.

Habitat: Shallow inlets, bays, and other inshore coastal waters.

Distribution: Two highly migratory populations survive from 72° north in the Arctic and north Pacific Oceans southward to Japan and Korea for the small western population, and as far south as Jalisco, Mexico, for the much larger eastern population known as California Gray Whales. The latter often are observed from headlands and cliffs along the Pacific coastline of the United States and Canada as well as from observation lookouts beside the famous calving lagoons in Baja California. The north Atlantic Ocean population is extinct.

Gray Whale blowing. Note barnacles and scars. (photo by William Rossiter).

Ziphiidae: Beaked Whales

The little-known, medium-sized toothed whales in this family reach lengths of 15 to 30 feet (5 to 9 meters) and are creatures of the open sea. The elongated jaws suggest a duck's bill; the lower jaw extends to or beyond the tip of the snout. The upper jaw lacks teeth; there are one or two pairs of teeth in the lower jaw. The throat furrows form a V. There is one blowhole. The dorsal fin is placed relatively far back toward the wide flukes which have little or no notch. The flippers are long and slender.

North Sea Beaked Whale *Mesoplodon bidens*   Plate 6
Other Name: Sowerby's Beaked Whale.
Length: 16 feet (4.8 meters).
Weight: 3,000 pounds (1,360 kilograms).
Description: A rare species with an unusually slender, streamlined
    dark charcoal-gray body and white spots and lines. Immatures
    lack the spots and are lighter on the belly. The head has an
    elongated beak, concave forehead, and a bulge ahead of the
    blowhole. There is one tooth on each lower jaw midway back
    from the snout; the tooth protrudes in the male and is visible
    from the outside. There is a relatively tall dorsal fin, triangular
    to falcate in shape. The flippers are rather long. The tips of the
    flukes are rounded, there is no notch, and the rear margin can
    be concave.
Food: Squid and occasionally fish.
Habitat: Deep oceanic waters.
Distribution: The north Atlantic Ocean from Newfoundland south
    to Massachusetts on the western side, and from Norway, the
    Baltic Sea, and the British Isles southward into the Mediter-
    ranean Sea on the eastern side.

Strap-Toothed Whale *Mesoplodon layardii*   Plate 6
Other Names: None.
Length: 16 feet (4.8 meters).
Weight: 2,800 pounds (1,270 kilograms).
Description: Dark gray on the back shaded to slate gray on the sides
    and off-white on the belly. The streamlined head is small with
    a bulge dipping down into the long snout. The body is com-
    pressed laterally. The lower jaw contains two flat teeth which
    grow out and over the outside of the upper jaw, thus producing
    a white strap-like appearance.
Food: Unknown.
Habitat: Deep oceanic and marine waters; occasionally coastal
    waters.
Distribution: Waters between the Falkland Islands and South Africa
    in the south Atlantic Ocean; also waters around New Zealand
    and southern Australia in the south Pacific and Indian Oceans.

Gulf Stream Beaked Whale   Plate 6
Mesoplodon (gervaisi) europaeus

Other Names: Antillean Beaked Whale, Gervais' Beaked Whale.
Length: 22 feet (6.6 meters).

Weight: 6,000 pounds (2,722 kilograms).
Description: A rare, little-known whale similar to *M. mirus* and *M. bidens* with a small head and laterally compressed body. The flippers are very narrow and small. The dorsal fin, variable in shape from falcate to triangular, is placed rather far back on the body. The dark-gray flukes are small with rounded tips. The species is dark grayish-black on the back and sides but lighter on the undersides. Many white lines (scars) mark the back and upper sides.
Food: Probably squid, cuttlefish, and other fish.
Habitat: Deep oceanic waters.
Distribution: In the English Channel and north Atlantic Ocean from New York southward to Florida; also in the Gulf of Mexico and the Caribbean Sea from Cuba southward to Trinidad.

True's Beaked Whale *Mesoplodon mirus*   Plate 6
Other Names: None.
Length: 17 feet (5.1 meters).
Weight: 3,000 pounds (1,361 kilograms).
Description: A very rare whale characterized by short jaws, a notable beak, a forehead bulge, and a shallow indentation near the blowhole. The head is small and streamlined. The black or dark-gray back fades to pale gray on the sides, and the abdomen is white marked with black flecks. The dorsal fin is positioned behind the midpoint on the back and has a notable ridge extending to the flukes. The small, black flippers are placed far forward and positioned vertically. The tips of the dark, broad flukes are rounded and sometimes there is a slight notch in the flukes. The species is very similar to Cuvier's Beaked Whale *(Ziphius cavirostris).*
Food: Squid and occasionally fish.
Habitat: Deep oceanic waters of the Gulf Stream.
Distribution: In the western north Atlantic Ocean from Cape Breton Island southward to Florida, and in the eastern north Atlantic Ocean off the British and French coasts; in the south Atlantic Ocean off South Africa's southern coast.

Camperdown Whale *Mesoplodon grayi*   Plate 7
Other Names: Southern Beaked Whale, Gray's Beaked Whale, New Zealand Scamperdown Whale.

Length: 13 feet (3.9 meters).

Weight: 1,700 pounds (771 kilograms).

Description: A rare whale with a grayish-green back and a brownish-green abdomen. The sharply pointed and triangular dorsal fin is positioned about two-thirds of the way back on the animal's backside. There are well-marked, V-shaped grooves on the lower surface of the body. The tips of the flukes are rounded, but the flukes lack a notch. Many white lines (scars) mark the body.

Food: Unknown. Probably squid and fish.

Habitat: Coastal waters.

Distribution: In the north Atlantic Ocean off the coast of the Netherlands; in the south Atlantic Ocean from the latitudes of the coast of Argentina and the Falkland Islands southward to South Africa; in the south Pacific Ocean from the coast of Chile southward to New Zealand; and in the Indian Ocean from South Africa to Australia.

Pacific Beaked Whale *Mesoplodon pacificus*   (Not illustrated)

Other Name: Longman's Beaked Whale.

Length: 23 feet (6.9 meters).

Weight: Unknown.

Description: Known with certainty only from a few skulls. It apparently is a large beaked whale which may be light to rust brown in color. The head perhaps is lighter with a slender beak. However, this description is speculative and is based upon the opinions of W. F. J. Mörzer Bruyns.

Food: Unknown.

Habitat: Perhaps deep waters.

Distribution: Off Australia (Queensland) and Somalia; also at 165° west longitude on the equator.

Hector's Beaked Whale *Mesoplodon hectori*   (Not illustrated)

Other Names: None.

Length: Information unavailable.

Weight: Information unavailable.

Description: Known only from a few skulls. The whale's external appearance is unknown. Probably it has a general resemblance to the other *Mesoplodon* whales.

Food: Unknown.

Habitat: Information unavailable.
Distribution: New Zealand waters.

Blainville's Beaked Whale *Mesoplodon densirostris*   Plate 7

Other Name: Dense-beaked Whale.
Length: 17 feet (5.2 meters).
Weight: 2,400 pounds (1,089 kilograms).
Description: A rare black or charcoal-gray whale with the abdomen
    dark gray. Various white blotches and scars mark the body
    which is spindle-shaped. The head was a gape rise and the
    mouth an arching contour in adult males especially. An out-
    growth of a tooth protrudes from each side of the lower jaw
    which, in males, is distinctive. The triangular to falcate dorsal
    fin is placed about three-quarters of the way back on the back-
    side. The small flippers are narrow. The flukes, light below
    and dark above, rarely are notched; sometimes they extend
    slightly backward near the center.
Food: Squid.
Habitat: Deep marine and ocean waters.
Distribution: In the north Atlantic Ocean from offshore Nova Scotia
    southward to the Bahama Islands on the western side, and
    from offshore Madeira Islands and South Africa on the eastern
    side; in the western Pacific Ocean off Queensland, Australia,
    and the Lord Howe Islands; in the north Pacific Ocean off
    Midway Island; in the Indian Ocean from the Seychelles
    Islands off East Africa and South Africa (Algoa Bay) south-
    ward to western Australia.

Stejneger's Beaked Whale *Mesoplodon stejnegeri*   Plate 7

Other Name: Saber-Toothed Whale.
Length: 16 feet (4.8 meters).
Weight: 2,800 pounds (1,270 kilograms).
Description: A rare, black whale with a spindle-shaped body. There
    is a pair of triangular-shaped teeth in the lower jaw. The teeth
    in males are considerably larger than in females. The flukes
    lack a notch, but the tips are pointed. Numerous white scars
    mark the body. There also are round white spots on the body.
Food: Unknown. Probably squid and fish.
Habitat: Deep ocean waters.
Distribution: The north Pacific Ocean from the Bering Sea south-

ward to Oregon on the eastern side and Japan on the western side.

Japanese Beaked Whale *Mesoplodon ginkgodens*   Plate 9

Other Names: Ginkgo Whale, Ginkgo-Toothed Beaked Whale.
Length: 17 feet (5.1 meters).
Weight: 3,200 pounds (1,452 kilograms).
Description: A very rare streamlined whale with a black or dark-gray back and sides shading to a gray abdomen. The long beak merges with the head. A flap of skin on the lower jaw touches the upper jaw. There is a small dorsal fin placed about two-thirds of the way along the back. There are narrow, small flippers and large tail flukes lacking a notch. There are white spots scattered over the body.
Food: Fish such as salmon.
Habitat: Shallow coastal and marine waters.
Distribution: The north Pacific Ocean in Japanese waters on the western side, and California (near San Diego) waters on the eastern side; also the Indian Ocean in Ceylon waters.

Bowdoini's Beaked Whale   (Not illustrated)
Mesoplodon bowdoini

Other Names: Andrew's Whale, Andrew's Beaked Whale.
Length: Information unavailable.
Weight: Information unavailable.
Description: Similar in appearance to Stejneger's Beaked Whale with which it has been confused at times.
Food: Unknown.
Habitat: Unknown.
Distribution: The south Pacific and Indian Oceans from New Zealand to the waters of western Australia.

Hubb's Beaked Whale *Mesoplodon carlhubbsi*   Plate 9

Other Name: Hubb's Whale.
Length: 16.7 feet (5 meters).
Weight: Information unavailable.
Description: A very rare gray whale with a small dorsal fin positioned two-thirds of the way back on the body. The small flippers are elongated.
Food: Unknown. Probably squid and fish.

Habitat: Unknown.

Distribution: Confined to the north Pacific Ocean between latitudes 32° north and 47° north on the eastern side, and along the coast of Japan on the western side.

Cuvier's Beaked Whale *Ziphius cavirostris*   Plate 7

Other Names: Goosebeaked Whale, Cuvier's Whale.

Length: 23 feet (6.9 meters).

Weight: 11,000 pounds (4,990 kilograms).

Description: A streamlined whale with a small head, an indistinct beak in larger individuals, and a back indentation behind the head. The blowhole is placed on top of the head and far forward. Males have a pair of teeth at the tip of the lower jaw; the teeth do not show in females. The body varies in color from dark rust brown to dark slate gray (occasionally creamy white) above and gray below. A few individuals have pale gray backs. Old males are distinctively white-headed. The tall and distinct dorsal fin is located far behind the midpoint on the back. White scars mark the bodies of all individuals. The flukes are dark below. Forms pods of up to 25 individuals.

Food: Squid and fish.

Habitat: Very deep ocean waters.

Distribution: In the north Atlantic Ocean from the Mediterranean north to the Baltic and North Seas on the eastern side, and on the western side from the West Indies and Florida north to Rhode Island and Massachusetts; in the south Atlantic Ocean off South Africa and Argentina; in the eastern north Pacific Ocean from the Bering Sea southward to Baja California, and in the western Pacific Ocean from eastern Siberia south to Japan and the waters off the Hawaiian and Midway Islands; in the western south Pacific Ocean from New Ireland (Bismarck Archipelago) to New Zealand and Australia, and in the eastern south Pacific Ocean off Chile; in the Indian Ocean from South Africa southward to Australia.

Southern Beaked Whale *Berardius arnuxii*   Plate 8

Other Names: Arnoux Beaked Whale, Arnoux Whale.

Length: 32 feet (9.6 meters).

Weight: 17,000 pounds (7,711 kilograms).

Description: A rather large-headed whale with a narrow, pointed snout, large flippers, and wide flukes. The body is dark blue-gray above, mottled on the sides, and pale gray below. There are two pairs of teeth in both sexes. Numerous scars mark the body.

Food: Squid and fish.

Habitat: Deep coastal and marine waters.

Distribution: Confined to the south Pacific, south Atlantic, and Indian Oceans from latitude 33° south to the Antarctic pack ice. Concentrations occur around the Falkland Islands, coastal South America, New Zealand, and Australia.

Baird's Beaked Whale *Berardius bairdii*   Plate 8

Other Name: Giant Bottlenose Whale.

Length: 40 feet (12 meters).

Weight: 24,000 pounds (10,886 kilograms).

Description: A long beaked whale with well-marked, V-shaped grooves on the throat. The flippers are small and the fluke medium in size. The body is gray, somewhat paler on the under parts. The small dorsal fin is triangular and placed on the back near the tail. The lower jaw contains two pairs of teeth. Whitish patches occur on the throat, behind the flippers, and on the belly. Can be confused with Minke Whales, but Baird's Beaked Whales often occur in pods of up to 20 animals.

Food: Squid and a few fish.

Habitat: Coastal and marine waters.

Distribution: In the north Pacific Ocean from the Bering Sea southward to Japan on the western side, and from the Bering Sea southward to Monterey Bay, California, on the eastern side.

Tasmanian Beaked Whale *Tasmacetus shepherdi*   Plate 8

Other Name: Shepherd's Beaked Whale.

Length: 30 feet (9 meters).

Weight: 5,400 pounds (2,500 kilograms).

Description: A very rare black or dark-brown whale with pale undersides and short, well-toothed jaws within a pointed snout.

Food: Presumably squid and fish.

Habitat: Apparently oceanic waters.

Distribution: Waters around New Zealand, Chile, and Argentina.

Northern Bottlenose Whale *Hyperoodon ampullatus*   Plate 9

Other Name: Bottlenosed Whale.

Length: 33 feet (9.9 meters).

Weight: 18,000 pounds (8,165 kilograms).

Description: A dark gray or brownish whale with a large, bulbous head (especially in males). The long, bottle-shaped jaws have one pair of teeth on the lower jaws. The blowhole is placed behind the head above the eyes. The dorsal fin is small and placed two-thirds of the way back on the body; it is sickle-shaped with the tip pointing backward. The flippers are relatively modest in size. The spout reaches 2 feet (0.6 meters) in height.

Food: Squid.

Habitat: Deep ocean waters.

Distribution: Arctic seas south to Rhode Island and the Mediterranean in the north Atlantic Ocean; in the north Pacific Ocean in Arctic waters from the Bering Sea southward to Japan.

Southern Bottlenose Whale   (Not illustrated)
Hyperoodon planifrons

Other Names: None.

Length: 25 feet (7.5 meters).

Weight: 7,000 pounds (3,175 kilograms).

Description: Similar to the Northern Bottlenose Whale but blue-black blending to pale blue-gray on the undersides. Compared with the Northern Bottlenose Whale, the bulge on the forehead is more pronounced, the dorsal fin is placed closer to the tail, and the flukes are somewhat larger.

Food: Squid.

Habitat: Probably deep ocean waters.

Distribution: From the Antarctic pack ice (77°32' south, 173°22' west) northward to 39° south latitude in the south Atlantic Ocean, 20° south latitude in the Indian Ocean, and 33° south latitude in the south Pacific Ocean.

Physeteridae: Sperm Whales

These whales are separated into three species placed in two genera. The largest, the Sperm Whale, is the creature featured in Herman Melville's *Moby Dick*. It is the largest cetacean with teeth, which are especially notable in the lower jaw. Ambergris, the peculiar substance used in perfume, medicine, and other products, is derived from Sperm Whales. Spermaceti oil also comes from these animals.

Sperm Whale *Physeter catodon*   Plate 10

Other Name: Cachalot.

Length: 69 feet (20.9 meters).

Weight: 120,000 pounds (54,432 kilograms).

Description: A very large, dark, brownish whale with a massive head forming about one-third of the animal's total length. Creamy-white individuals also are known. The snout is nearly square and is distinctive. The blowhole is positioned on the left side of the head near the tip and produces an impressive, distinctive spout extending forward about 45° and rising about 45 feet (15 meters) into the air. There is a rounded dorsal hump positioned two-thirds of the distance along the back; it is followed by various midline knuckles. The body appears shriveled. The flippers are not especially large. The triangular flukes are broad with a deep notch on the rear edge. Sperm Whales are reported in numbers ranging from 1 to 50 individuals.

Food: Squid, octopus, sharks, and fish.

Habitat: Deep coastal and marine waters; oceanic during migrations, usually within 300 miles of shore and in water at least 600 feet (182.9 meters) deep.

Distribution: The tropical, temperate, and polar seas of the world.

Pygmy Sperm Whale *Kogia breviceps*   Plate 10

Other Name: Dwarf Sperm Whale.

Length: 11 feet (3.4 meters).

Weight: 1,500 pounds (680 kilograms).

Description: A rare, robust whale with a shark-like head, dark steel-gray back, lighter gray sides, and dull white belly. The narrow lower jaw is underslung and positioned far behind the snout, and there is a crescent-shaped false gill present. The small dorsal fin is backcurved and placed on the posterior portion of the back. The flippers and flukes are steel gray on the upper side.

Food: Squid and fish.

Habitat: Deep waters.

Distribution: Occurs in the eastern Atlantic Ocean off the coasts of
the Netherlands, France, and South Africa; in the western
north Atlantic Ocean from Nova Scotia south to Florida and
off Texas; in the eastern Pacific Ocean off southern Peru, and
from Mexico (Mazatlán) north to Washington; in the western
Pacific Ocean off Japan, the South and East China Seas, and
New Zealand and Australia; off Hawaii in the central Pacific
Ocean; and in the Indian Ocean from South Africa to
Australia.

Dwarf Sperm Whale *Kogia simus*   Plate 10

Other Name: Rat Porpoise.
Length: 9 feet (2.7 meters).
Weight: Information unavailable.
Description: An unusually robust whale colored dark steel gray on
the back, the sides lighter gray, and a dull white belly. The
head is blunted, and false gill marks are present on the sides of
the head. The tall dorsal fin is backcurved. Otherwise it is
more or less similar to the Pygmy Sperm Whale with which it
sometimes is confused.
Food: Squid and fish.
Habitat: Ocean waters.
Distribution: The north Atlantic Ocean from Georgia southward to
St. Vincent in the Caribbean and the northeastern portion of
the Gulf of Mexico. Perhaps also parts of the Pacific Ocean
as well.

Monodontidae: White Whales

The two species in this family (subfamily of some authors) lack a
beak and dorsal fin and apparently are related to the dolphins. Both
species have Arctic distributions.

White Whale *Delphinapterus leucas*   Plate 11

Other Names: Beluga, Beluga Whale, Sea Canary, White Porpoise.
Length: 18 feet (5.4 meters).
Weight: 2,400 pounds (1,088 kilograms).
Description: The adult is white to creamy in color (6 years old or
older) with robust bodies, a notable neck area, and a small
head. Calves are dark brown; immatures are slate gray before
developing the adult coloration. It is a beautiful whale lacking

a dorsal fin but with a notched dorsal ridge. It is noted for its ability to swim slowly with undulating movements.

Food: Fish (especially cod), squid, crabs, mollusks, and other items.

Habitat: Coastal waters; sometimes swims for miles up rivers.

Distribution: Restricted to the Arctic seas of North America and Eurasia. In the north Pacific Ocean from 81° north latitude southward to Alaska and Japan; in the eastern north Atlantic Ocean southward to the British Isles and France (Bay of Biscay); in the western north Atlantic Ocean southward to Massachusetts.

Narwhal *Monodon monoceros*   Plate 11

Other Names: Narwal, Narwhale, Unicorn Whale.

Length: 16 feet (4.9 meters).

Weight: 2,000 pounds (907 kilograms).

Description: A distinctive whale, brownish-gray above and white below, with grayish-black spots on the back, sides, and flukes. Young individuals are dark bluish-gray. In the male the left tooth (rarely both teeth) erupts into a long spiraled tusk reaching lengths of up to 10 feet (3 meters), thus giving the creature a unique appearance among whales. The function of the tusk is unknown. Narwhals lack a dorsal fin.

Food: Squid, crabs, and fish (flounder, rockfish, and cod).

Habitat: Open seas between pack ice; also marine and coastal areas.

Distribution: Restricted to the Arctic seas of the Atlantic and Pacific Oceans. In the eastern Atlantic Ocean southward to the Netherlands and the British Isles; in the western Atlantic Ocean southward to Labrador; in the Pacific Ocean southward to the Bering Sea.

Delphinidae (in part): Killer, False Killer, Pygmy Killer and Pilot Whales

These species are oceanic dolphins with conspicuous triangular dorsal fins, teeth on both jaws, no throat grooves, and notched flukes. The larger species in the family (those discussed here) are called whales for practical purposes.

Pygmy Killer Whale *Feresa attenuata*   Plate 12

Other Name: Pygmy Killer.

Length: 8 feet (2.4 meters).

Weight: 350 pounds (159 kilograms).

Description: Black or dark gray with light gray sides. The dorsal fin is high, well defined, and in the center of the back. The lips and chin are white as is the underside area around the genitals. The tips of the flippers are slightly rounded. The species typically stands in an upright posture with the head above waterline which enables it to look around. It can be aggressive at which time it slaps the water with the flukes and flippers, engages in jaw snapping, and even growls warning sounds.

Food: Sardines.

Habitat: Deep coastal, marine, and ocean waters.

Distribution: Waters off Japan (Honshu) in the north Pacific Ocean; in Hawaiian waters in the central Pacific Ocean; and off the Senegal coast in the north Atlantic Ocean.

Pod of Killer Whales (photo by Jeffrey Goodyear).

Killer Whale *Orcinus orca* Plate 12

Other Name: Orca.

Length: 30 feet (9 meters).

Weight: 16,000 pounds (7,258 kilograms).

Description: A boldly marked and robust black-and-white whale with striking white areas above the eye, a gray saddle behind the dorsal fin, and white on the undersides including the flukes. In males the pointed, erect dorsal fin reaches a height of about 6 feet (1.8 meters); in immature males and females it is only about 3 feet (0.9 meters) high. Females are somewhat smaller than males. Killer Whales frequently expose their heads vertically out of the water to look around. Sometimes they breach completely out of the water. They may travel in pods of up to 50 individuals.

Food: Seals, some whales, dolphins, fish, sharks, squid, and octopus. There is one authentic record of an attack on a man.

Habitat: Generally deep coastal and marine waters, but occasionally shallow waters.

Distribution: Widely distributed in the world's seas from the Antarctic (including the coasts of Antarctica) to the Arctic. In the western south Atlantic Ocean northward to Buenos Aires, Argentina (38°50′ S.); in the western north Atlantic Ocean southward to the Bahamas and Florida; in the eastern south Pacific Ocean northward to coastal Chile (37° S.); in the eastern north Pacific Ocean from Alaska southward to Costa Rica.

Alula Whale *Orcinus mörzer-bruynsus*   Plate 12

Other Name: Alula Killer.

Length: 24 feet (7.2 meters).

Weight: 4,000 pounds (1,814 kilograms).

Description: A sepia brown *Orcinus* whale with a well-rounded forehead and white, star-like scars on the body. The dorsal fin, about 2 feet (0.6 meters) high, is prominent and often protrudes well above the surface of the water. This species was discussed and illustrated for the first time, but not formally named, by W. F. J. Mörzer Bruyns in *Field Guide of Whales and Dolphins*.

Food: Information unavailable.

Habitat: Deep coastal waters.

Distribution: Eastern Gulf of Aden to Socotra.

False Killer Whale *Pseudorca crassidens*   Plate 13

Other Names: False Killer, Lesser Killer Whale.

Length: 20 feet (6 meters).

Weight: 4,800 pounds (2,177 kilograms).

Description: Entirely black with a blunt head and conspicuous dorsal fin.

Food: Squid and fish.

Habitat: Usually deep waters, but occasionally coastal waters.

Distribution: In the eastern Atlantic Ocean from the Baltic and North Seas southward to the Mediterranean and the Cape of Good Hope; in the western Atlantic Ocean from New Jersey south through the Caribbean to Argentina (Buenos Aires); in the eastern Pacific Ocean from Washington south to Mexico

(Guerrero) and Peru (Paita); in the western Pacific Ocean from Japan south to Australia and New Zealand; and in the Indian Ocean around Ceylon and off India.

Little Killer *Peponocephala electra*   Plate 13

Other Names: Broad-Backed Dolphin, Many-Toothed Blackfish, Melon-Headed Whale, and Hawaiian Blackfish.

Length: 9 feet (2.7 meters).

Weight: 400 pounds (181 kilograms).

Description: A very rare, slim, elongated species. It is black on the back, lighter on the bottom, with white lips and a light area between the flippers and around the genital slit. There is no beak, a rounded forehead, and the head suggests a False Killer Whale.

Food: Probably fish.

Habitat: Oceanic and marine waters.

Distribution: Confined to tropical seas north of 10° south latitude, including the coasts of India, Hawaii, Senegal, Guinea, Madras, and Indonesia. Not recorded in South American waters.

Atlantic Pilot Whale *Globicephala melaena*   Plate 13

Other Names: Blackfish, Pothead.

Length: 20 feet (6.2 meters).

Weight: 8,400 pounds (3,810 kilograms).

Description: Black with a bulbous head (extremely so in adult males), a round-tipped dorsal fin with a long base located forward on the back, and long, narrow, sickle-shaped flippers measuring one-fifth the length of the animal. There is a gray, anchor-shaped area on the chin and a gray belly area. A gray saddle behind the dorsal fin is reported on some large individuals. Usually, it is reported in herds of 4 to 6 animals, but occasionally up to 50 are seen and rarely 200 or more appear. May associate with Atlantic White-Sided Dolphins. Spyhopping sometimes is done, but breaching is infrequent.

Food: Squid and fish.

Habitat: Coastal waters and along the edges of the continental shelf in waters deeper than 100 fathoms.

Distribution: In the western north Atlantic Ocean, in winter, from the Grand Banks southward to North Carolina with concentrations near Cape Cod and coastal Newfoundland; in summer from Iceland and Greenland southward to coastal New Jersey; in the eastern Atlantic Ocean from Norway south to the Cape of Good Hope.

Short-Finned Pilot Whale
Globicephala macrorhynchus

Plate 13

Other Name: Blackfish.

Length: 17.5 feet (5.3 meters).

Weight: 7,350 pounds (3,307 kilograms).

Description: A black whale with a gray patch on the chin and belly. Similar to the Atlantic Pilot Whale with a thick, bulbous head (squarish in mature males). The melon sometimes overhangs the mouth in unusually old males. The dorsal fin, placed forward on the back, has a long base and a low profile. The sickle-shaped flippers measure about one-sixth the body length (compared with one-fifth in the Atlantic Pilot Whale). Reported in herds of 60 or more but generally fewer individuals are seen.

Food: Squid and fish.

Habitat: Coastal and marine waters.

Distribution: In the western north Atlantic Ocean from New Jersey (Delaware Bay)—but usually Virginia (summer) or North Carolina—southward past Bermuda to waters off Venezuela; the Gulf of Mexico; and the Caribbean and its islands.

Atlantic Pilot Whale's melon, blowhole, back, and dorsal fin. (photo by Jeffrey Goodyear).

Pacific Pilot Whale *Globicephala scammonii*   Plate 13

Other Name: Pacific Blackfish.
Length: 18 feet (5.4 meters).
Weight: 7,560 pounds (3,402 kilograms).
Description: A black or brownish-gray whale with a faint grayish
        saddle behind the dorsal fin and a narrow, gray belly stripe.
        The forehead or melon is bulbous and the slippers are long and
        sickle-shaped. The dorsal fin has a wide base, is relatively low,
        and has a rounded tip (conspicuously hooked in adults). The
        whale moves slowly with 5 to 50 (or more) individuals some-
        times reported.
Food: Squid and fish.
Habitat: Coastal and marine waters.
Distribution: In the eastern Pacific Ocean from Alaska southward to
        Peru; in the western Pacific Ocean from Japan southward to
        New Zealand.

Platanistidae: River Dolphins

These primitive dolphins are subject to different taxonomic
treatment by various authorities. They are largely freshwater species.
Relatively little is known about some of them.

Ganges Dolphin *Platanista gangetica*   Plate 14

Other Names: Ganges River Dolphin, Susu.
Length: 8 feet (2.4 meters).
Weight: 150 pounds (73 kilograms).
Description: A blind, grayish-black dolphin with a long, thin beak
        and a rounded forehead. A triangular dorsal fin is located
        approximately midway on the back. Echolocation is used to
        navigate in the muddy rivers in which it lives. The species is
        endangered.
Food: Shrimp and fish.
Habitat: Muddy waters where strong currents occur.
Distribution: The Ganges-Brahmaputra Rivers in Assam, India, and
        Pakistan; the Hooghly River in India (Bengal); and the Indus
        in northwestern India (Sutley River), and western Pakistan
        from tidewater to the Himalayas.

Amazon River Dolphin *Inia geoffrensis*   Plate 14

Other Names: Amazon Dolphin, Pink Porpoise, Boto.

Length: 9 feet (2.7 meters).

Weight: 240 pounds (109 kilograms).

Description: A pinkish-gray dolphin with a long, thin beak and a rounded forehead. The dorsal ridge and hump and outer edges of the flukes are notably paler pink than the sides of the body when the animal dives. They often surface exposing the back and occasionally breach out of the water. They are not uncommon in the Amazon basin. The species sometimes associates with the Tucuxi Dolphin which also lives in the Amazon basin.

Food: Fish.

Habitat: Fast-flowing rivers in the midstream as well as placid lakes and lagoons.

Distribution: The Amazon River and its many tributaries in Brazil, Bolivia, Peru, Ecuador, Colombia, and Venezuela. Also occurs in the Casiquiare Canal, upper Rio Orinoco, and Rio Guaviare in Colombia.

Chinese Lake Dolphin *Lipotes vexillifer*   Plate 14

Other Names: Whiteflag Dolphin, Pei Chi.

Length: 9 feet (2.7 meters).

Weight: 180 pounds (82 kilograms).

Description: A chunky dolphin, grayish to blue-gray above and white below, with a typical long, slender beak and a low dorsal fin. The rectangular blowhole is placed on the left side of the head.

Food: Catfish and other bottom-dwelling aquatic life.

Habitat: The waters of Tungting Lake and the Yangtze Kiang River in Hunan, China.

Distribution: Tungting Lake and the Yangtze Kiang River in Hunan, China.

La Plata Dolphin *Pontoporia blainvillei*   Plate 14

Other Name: Franciscana.

Length: About 6 feet (1.8 meters).

Weight: 90 pounds (41 kilograms).

Description: A small, pale, gray-brown dolphin somewhat darker above and lighter below. The species has an unusually long, narrow beak. The dorsal fin is rather tall with a long base. The large flippers are triangular.

Food: Fish and invertebrates.

Habitat: Coastal waters and those of the La Plata River delta.
Distribution: The delta of La Plata River and the Atlantic coast of
South America from Rio Grande do Sul (Brazil) south to Pe-
ninsula Valdés (Argentina).

Stenidae: Dolphins

The species in this family can be separated into five major
groups based upon their preferred habitats: (1) ocean or pelagic dolphins, (2) marine dolphins which occur to within 150 to 200 miles
(240 to 320 kilometers) of the coast, (3) coastal dolphins which venture up to 50 miles (80 kilometers) offshore, (4) estuary dolphins
which live in entrances to rivers and shallow coastlines up to 2 miles
(3.2 kilometers) offshore, and (5) river dolphins which venture up
rivers for varying distances.

Rough-Toothed Dolphin *Steno bredanensis*   Plate 17

Other Names: Rough-Toothed Porpoise, Goggle-Eyed Porpoise.
Length: 8 feet (2.4 meters).
Weight: 350 pounds (159 kilograms).
Description: Variable in color from dark gray to dark purplish-gray
on the back. Sides and belly blotches are pinkish-white and the
belly is white. The flippers and flukes are dark. The long, slender beak is white or pinkish-white on the sides and the forehead slopes into the rostrum. There is no transverse groove
between the forehead and beak. Reported in groups of up to
50 individuals.
Food: Unknown.
Haibtat: Deep coastal waters such as those off the edge of the continental shelf.
Distribution: In the eastern north Atlantic Ocean from the Netherlands south to Portugal, and off the Ivory Coast and Senegal;
in the western north Atlantic from Virginia south to Florida
and Cuba; in the south Atlantic Ocean from the northern coast
of Brazil to Tristan da Cunha; in the north Pacific Ocean off
California, Hawaii, and Japan; in the south and equatorial
Pacific Ocean among the Galapagos Islands; in the Indian
Ocean from the gulf of Aden and Mossel Bay, South Africa, to
Java and the Bay of Bengal.

Tucuxi Dolphin *Sotalia fluviatilis*   Plate 15

Other Names: Bufeo, Bouto, Amazon River Dolphin.
Length: 6 feet (1.8 meters).
Weight: 90 pounds (41 kilograms).
Description: A grayish dolphin with a pinkish lower jaw and throat
    and whitish undersides. The dorsal fin is higher and more
    triangular than exhibited by the Amazon River Dolphin (*Inia*).
    Often associates with the more common Amazon River Dol-
    phin in tropical Amazonia.
Food: Fish.
Habitat: River waters.
Distribution: The Amazon River and its tributaries between the
    Para channels above Belem and the Rio Huallaga in Peru.

Guiana River Dolphin *Sotalia guianensis*   Plate 15

Other Name: Guiana Dolphin.
Length: 5.6 feet (1.7 meters).
Weight: 100 pounds (45 kilograms).
Description: A steel blue to dark brown dolphin with a white belly.
    The dorsal fin is prominent and nearly triangular with the tip
    curving slightly backward. A brownish band may appear on
    the sides. Reported in groups of up to about 8.
Food: Fish.
Habitat: Coastal rivers; also brackish and salt waters.
Distribution: Coastlines and rivers of the Guianas and Venezuela in-
    cluding Lake Maracaibo.

Rio de Janeiro Dolphin *Sotalia brasiliensis*   (Not illustrated)

Other Name: Brazilian Dolphin.
Length: About 6 feet (1.8 meters).
Weight: Information unavailable.
Description: Very similar (perhaps conspecific?) to the Tucuxi
    Dolphin.
Food: Presumably fish.
Habitat: Coastal waters.
Distribution: Rio de Janeiro Bay.

Chinese White Dolphin *Sousa chinensis*   Plate 16

Other Names: None.
Length: 6 feet (1.8 meters).

Weight: 120 pounds (54 kilograms).
Description: An ivory-white, light gray, or pink dolphin with dark
   eyes. *S. borneensis,* described by some authorities as a separate
   species, is considered here as conspecific with *S. chinensis.*
Food: Fish.
Habitat: River entrances and inshore coastal waters.
Distribution: The China Seas and Chinese coastline from Sarawak
   north into the Canton and Fuchow Rivers; also ventures at
   least 750 miles up the Yangtze to Hankow.

Speckled Dolphin *Sousa lentiginosa*   Plate 16

Other Names: None.
Length: 6 feet (1.8 meters).
Weight: 120 pounds (54 kilograms).
Description: Gray with pinkish or whitish blotches. The small dor-
   sal fin is placed on a dorsal ridge. The broad flippers have
   square-cut ends.
Food: Fish.
Habitat: Salt and brackish waters and muddy coastal and river
   waters.
Distribution: In the Bay of Bengal from Ceylon to Madras and west-
   ward to South African waters.

Plumbeous Dolphin *Sousa plumbea*   Plate 16

Other Names: Lead-Colored Dolphin, Malabar Dolphin.
Length: 9 feet (2.7 meters).
Weight: About 200 pounds (91 kilograms).
Description: Light gray heavily marked with small white spots over
   most of the body. The small white dorsal fin rests on a long
   dorsal ridge. The lower jaw is white, as is the forepart of the
   upper jaw. The rear portions of the flukes also are white.
Food: Fish.
Habitat: Shallow brackish or salt coastal and river waters.
Distribution: Along the Sarawak coast in the South China Sea west-
   ward through the Straits of Malacca into the Bay of Bengal,
   and in the Red and Arabian Seas to the Suez Canal.

Cameroon Dolphin *Sousa teuszii*   Plate 15

Other Name: Cameroon River Dolphin.
Length: 7 feet (2.1 meters).

Weight: 190 pounds (86 kilograms).

Description: A rare brownish dolphin with a long dorsal ridge upon which rests the dorsal fin. The snout is long as in other *Sousa* dolphins.

Food: Fish.

Habitat: Inshore coastal waters and river entrances.

Distribution: The coastline of West Africa and the mouths of rivers from Senegal to the Cameroons.

Blue Dolphin *Stenella coeruleoalba* Plate 16

Other Names: Blue-White Dolphin, Striped Dolphin, Gray's Dolphin, Meyen's Dolphin, Striped Porpoise.

Length: 9 feet (2.7 meters).

Weight: 150 pounds (68 kilograms).

Description: A dark gray dolphin on its back with lighter gray sides and white underparts. A narrow black line (visible when the animal jumps out of the water) extends from the eye to a point near the anus, and another line runs from the eye to the flipper. Sometimes seen in herds of several hundred individuals.

Food: Fish.

Habitat: Coastal and marine waters.

Distribution: In the western Atlantic Ocean from southern Greenland south to Jamaica in the Caribbean and in the vicinity of Rio de La Plata, Argentina (35° south latitude); in the eastern Atlantic Ocean from the North Sea southward to the African seas; in the eastern Pacific Ocean from the Bering Sea south to the waters off Los Angeles, California; in the western Pacific Ocean in waters off Siberia, Japan, and New Zealand.

Long-Beaked Dolphin *Stenella longirostris* Plate 17

Other Names: Spinner Dolphin, Galapagos Dolphin, Arabian Dolphin, Spinner Porpoise.

Length: 7 feet (2.1 meters).

Weight: 200 pounds (91 kilograms).

Description: A slender dolphin with a dark gray to black back, tan to yellowish-brown on the sides, and white below. The short to long and slender beak is dark above and white below with the tip and lips black. The triangular (males) to falcate dorsal fin is lighter gray in the middle and dark gray or black on the border. The animal spins during leaps from the water. Reported in herds of several hundred, and readily rides bow waves of ships.

Food: Squid and fish.

Habitat: Ocean waters; sometimes coastal waters.

Distribution: In the eastern Pacific Ocean from the Tres Marias
Islands off Nayarit, Mexico, southward to Cape Horn and in
the western Pacific Ocean from Japan to Australia; in the western Atlantic Ocean from the Bahamas to the Gulf of Mexico,
and from Brazil to Cape Horn; in the eastern Atlantic Ocean
from Senegal to the Cape of Good Hope (South Africa); in the
Indian Ocean in Ceylon waters. The species seems to be especially common in the central Pacific Ocean between 100°
west and the Tunamontu Islands.

Narrow-Snouted Dolphin *Stenella graffmani*   Plate 18

Other Names: Gulf of Panama Spotted Dolphin, Graffman's Porpoise.

Length: 7 feet (2.1 meters).

Weight: 280 pounds (127 kilograms).

Description: A dark-brown species with numerous white spots on
the back and sides and paler patches on the sides. The small
dorsal fin is rather pointed at the tip.

Food: Fish.

Habitat: Along the continental shelf within 100-fathom waters.

Distribution: The eastern Pacific Ocean from Acapulco, Mexico,
south along the coast to Panama, and the west coast of Colombia (Isla Gorgona).

Atlantic Spotted Dolphin *Stenella plagiodon*   Plate 17

Other Names: Gulf Stream Spotted Dolphin, Spotter.

Length: 7.5 feet (2.3 meters).

Weight: 280 pounds (127 kilograms).

Description: A robust blackish-gray dolphin, somewhat lighter on
the sides, with numerous small grayish-white spots on the back
and sides and dark spots on the undersides. There is white on
the lips and beak. Immatures are purplish-gray or dark gray on
the back but do not have spots. The dorsal fin is large and
pointed at the tip. The flippers and rear edge of the flukes are
darker than the body coloration. Reported in herds of 50 to
several hundred individuals. They frequently ride bow waves
of ships.

Food: Squid, fish, and small eels.

Habitat: Coastal and marine waters generally within the 100-fathom depth but more than 5 miles (8 kilometers) offshore.

Distribution: In the north Atlantic Ocean from Cape Hatteras, North Carolina, (rarely north to Cape May, New Jersey) southward through the Gulf of Mexico and Caribbean Sea. In the south Atlantic Ocean off coastal Brazil.

Bridled Dolphin *Stenella attenuata*   Plate 17

Other Names: Bridled Spotted Dolphin, Bridled Porpoise.

Length: 7 feet (2.1 meters).

Weight: 250 pounds (113 kilograms).

Description: A short-beaked dark grayish or brownish dolphin, paler on the sides, with grayish-white spots on the back and sides. The lips are white or pinkish, there is a mouth-to-flipper stripe, and a distinct border separates the back and sides. The flukes and dorsal fin are black. Reported in herds of 5 to 30 individuals.

Food: Squid and fish.

Habitat: Deep waters.

Distribution: The eastern Atlantic Ocean from the vicinity of the Cape Verde Islands south to the Cape of Good Hope (South Africa); in the western Atlantic Ocean from North Carolina to Florida; the Gulf of Mexico and the Caribbean; off the coast of Venezuela; and apparently also in Japanese waters in the Pacific Ocean.

Delphinidae: Common Dolphins

The species in this family generally are the well-known dolphins which often swim with ships. They are easily observed.

Common Dolphin *Delphinus delphis*   Plate 18

Other Names: Atlantic Common Dolphin, Eastern Mediterranean Common Dolphin, White-Bellied Porpoise, Saddleback Dolphin.

Length: 8.5 feet (2.5 meters).

Weight: 300 pounds (136 kilograms).

Description: A bluish-gray or bluish-brown dolphin with a tan and pale yellowish-tan hourglass side pattern, a white beak, and white flippers. The black dorsal fin is triangular to falcate with a gray area in the center. The flukes are dark. Various subspecies differ somewhat in color patterns. Sometime seen in herds numbering 2,000 or more animals. Readily rides bow waves of ships.

Food: Squid and fish.

Habitat: Coastal and marine waters, in about 100-fathom depth, from 3 to 5 miles (4.8 to 8 kilometers) offshore.

Distribution: Widely distributed in various oceans and seas. In the western Atlantic Ocean from Newfoundland south to Jamaica, the Gulf of Mexico, and the coastlines of Brazil and Argentina; Tristan da Cunha; in the eastern Atlantic Ocean from Iceland, Norway, and the Baltic Sea into the African seas; the Indian Ocean; in the western south Pacific Ocean around Australia and New Zealand; in the eastern south Pacific Ocean in waters off Peru and Chile; in the north Pacific Ocean from the Bering and Okhotsk Seas south to Japan and Baja California; also the Black Sea.

Risso's Dolphin *Grampus griseus*   Plate 21

Other Name: Grampus Dolphin, Gray Grampus, White-Headed Grampus.

Length: 13 feet (3.9 meters).

Weight: 1,500 pounds (680 kilograms).

Description: A robust dolphin (ahead of the dorsal fin but narrow behind it) without a notable beak but with a bulbous head whose melon is divided into two parts by a crease. The tall dorsal fin, at midpoint on the back, is falcate. The dark flippers are long with pointed tips, and the flukes are broad, deeply notched, and concave along the rear edge. Newly born individuals are light gray, but adults are nearly black with grayish areas on the chest and belly. The head of old animals frequently is creamy white or silver-gray. Many scars mark the body. Sometimes seen in herds of a few hundred individuals.

Food: Squid and fish.

Habitat: Deep coastal waters beyond depths of 100 fathoms; marine and oceanic during migration.

Distribution: In the eastern Pacific Ocean from British Columbia south to Baja California and off Chile; in the western Pacific Ocean from Japan to Australian and New Zealand waters; the Indian Ocean and Red Sea; in the eastern Atlantic Ocean from Great Britain to the Mediterranean and Cape of Good Hope;

in the western Atlantic Ocean from Massachusetts south to Maryland.

Bottlenosed Dolphin *Turisops truncatus*   Plate 22

Other Names: Pacific Bottlenosed Dolphin, Bottlenosed Porpoise.
Length: 12 feet (3.6 meters).
Weight: 1,430 pounds (650 kilograms).
Description: A common, well-known dolphin whose back is dark gray, sides lighter gray, and belly white or pink with belly spots on old females. The lower jaw extends beyond the upper jaw. The tall, falcate dorsal fin has a broad base. Sometimes rides bow waves of ships.
Food: Fish (mullet, catfish, menhadden), shrimp, eels.
Habitat: The continental shelf in waters less than 100 fathoms, but often appears near shore in lagoons and bays and even swims up rivers to the limit of freshwater.
Distribution: Worldwide in temperate and tropical oceans and seas.

Pacific White-Sided Dolphin   Plate 19
Lagenorhynchus obliquidens

Other Name: White-Sided Dolphin.
Length: 8 feet (2.4 meters).
Weight: 300 pounds (136 kilograms).
Description: A black-and-white dolphin which exhibits great variability in color patterns. The high dorsal fin is black in front and white in the rear. Often associates with Common Dolphins in herds of as many as 2,000 individuals.
Food: Fish and squid.
Habitat: Coastal areas up to about 100 miles (160 kilometers) offshore.
Distribution: In the eastern Pacific Ocean from Alaska south to Baja California, and in the western Pacific Ocean from the Kuriles to Japan.

White-Beaked Dolphin *Lagenorhynchus albirostris* Plate 18

Other Names: White-Beaked Porpoise, Squidhound.
Length: 10 feet (3.1 meters).
Weight: 600 pounds (272 kilograms).
Description: A robust dolphin with a short light gray to white beak, dark gray to black back and sides (the latter with a pale area in

Risso's Dolphin's head, back, and dorsal fins (photo by Alan Brady).

front of and another behind the dorsal fin), a white to grayish belly, and a tall, dark-gray dorsal fin. Herds of 1,500 individuals are reported.

Food: Squid, octopus, herring, cod, capelin, and occasionally benthic crustacean.

Habitat: Oceanic and marine waters.

Distribution: The Arctic and north Atlantic Oceans south on the eastern side to Portugal and on the western side to Newfoundland.

Blackchin Dolphin *Lagenorhynchus australis* (Not illustrated)

Other Name: Peale's Porpoise.

Length: 6.5 feet (2 meters).

Weight: Information unavailable.

Description: A black-backed dolphin with a white belly, variable gray side patterns, black eyes, and black jaws. A black line extends from the mouth backward to the black flippers. The large, triangular dorsal fin is upright. The black flukes are notched. There is a long, narrow, white patch extending from the flippers to the flukes.

Food: Probably squid and fish.

Habitat: Offshore temperate waters.

Distribution: The western south Atlantic Ocean around the Falkland Islands and off southern South America.

Dusky Dolphin *Lagenorhynchus obscurus* Plate 21

Other Names: None.
Length: 8 feet (2.4 meters).
Weight: 300 pounds (136 kilograms).
Description: A black dolphin marked with variable patterns of gray
     and white. The high dorsal fin is black in front and grayish on
     the back portion.
Food: Fish and squid.
Habitat: Cool offshore waters.
Distribution: Temperate southern oceans.

Atlantic White-Sided Dolphin Plate 19
Lagenorhynchus acutus

Other Names: Atlantic White-Sided Porpoise, Jumper.
Length: 9 feet (2.7 meters).
Weight: 540 pounds (245 kilograms).
Description: A robust dolphin with a black beak and back, a white
     belly, and white, gray, and yellowish patches on the sides. The
     tall dorsal fin is partly black and partly gray. Reported in herds
     of up to 1,000 individuals, sometimes in association with Pilot
     Whales.
Food: Fish and squid.
Habitat: Oceanic and marine waters of moderate depth.
Distribution: The Arctic Ocean; in the eastern north Atlantic Ocean
     from the Barents Sea and Spitzbergen south to the Nether-
     lands and Great Britain, and in the western north Atlantic
     Ocean from Greenland south to Massachusetts.

Atlantic White-Sided Dolphin (photo by William Rossiter).

Hourglass Dolphin *Lagenorhynchus cruciger*   Plate 19

Other Names: None.
Length: 6 feet (1.8 meters).
Weight: 250 pounds (113 kilograms).
Description: A rare black and white dolphin with a high dorsal fin and a dark hourglass pattern on the sides of the body.
Food: Presumably fish.
Habitat: Antarctic waters in close proximity to pack ice.
Distribution: The south Atlantic Ocean from the Antarctic pack ice north to Rio de La Plata (35° south latitude); in the south Pacific Ocean from the Antarctic pack ice north to Atico (16° south latitude).

Sarawak Dolphin *Lagenodelphis hosei*   Plate 19

Other Names: Fraser's Dolphin, Bornean Dolphin.
Length: 8 feet (2.4 meters).
Weight: Unknown.
Description: A little-known robust dolphin, gray on the upper parts and white on the belly. A black side stripe extends from the rostrum back to the anus. The snout is short, and the flippers and dorsal fin are small. Sometimes reported in herds of 500 or more animals.
Food: Unknown.
Habitat: Offshore waters.
Distribution: Waters in the vicinity of the mouth of the Lutong River, Baram, Sarawak; eastern tropical Pacific Ocean; central Pacific Ocean; and near Australia, South Africa, and Japan. May occur elsewhere.

Commerson's Dolphin   Plate 20
Cephalorhynchus commersonii

Other Names: None.
Length: 5 feet (1.5 meters).
Weight: 120 pounds (54 kilograms).
Description: A short, fat dolphin with a largely white body but with the head-to-flippers area black and the dorsal fin-to-flukes area also black.
Food: Cuttlefish, krill, shrimp.
Habitat: Inshore waters such as fjord-like channels and bays in the Falkland Islands and Tierra del Fuego, South America.
Distribution: The south Atlantic Ocean from coastal Santa Cruz

to Tierra del Fuego and the Falkland Islands; in the south Pacific Ocean along Chile's southern coast; off Kerguelen Island in the Indian Ocean.

Hector's Dolphin *Cephalorhynchus hectori*   Plate 20

Other Name: Pied Hector's Dolphin.

Length: 5 feet (1.5 meters).

Weight: 120 pounds (54 kilograms).

Description: A white or gray dolphin with a black face stripe, black flippers, black dorsal fin, and black flukes and rear portion of the back.

Food: Small fish, cuttlefish, and shrimp.

Habitat: Shallow inshore waters, sometimes only 3 feet (0.9 meters) deep, at river bars, harbors, and deep bay entrances. Generally ventures no more than 2 miles (3.2 kilometers) offshore.

Distribution: The western Pacific Ocean from the South China Sea (Sarawak) to New Zealand.

Heaviside's Dolphin *Cephalorhynchus heavisidii*   Plate 20

Other Name: Heaviside Dolphin.

Length: 4 feet (1.2 meters).

Weight: 100 pounds (45 kilograms).

Description: A rare, small, black dolphin with notable white areas below on the flanks.

Food: Cuttlefish and shrimp.

Habitat: Presumably prefers cold inshore waters, especially along coastlines with fjord-like indentations.

Distribution: The south Atlantic and Indian Oceans off South Africa.

White-Bellied Dolphin *Cephalorhynchus eutropia*   Plate 20

Other Name: Chilean Dolphin.

Length: 4 feet (1.2 meters).

Weight: 120 pounds (54 kilograms).

Description: A rare, black dolphin with several white areas on the belly (not visible in the field).

Food: Cuttlefish and shrimp.

Habitat: Inshore waters.

Distribution: Restricted to the south Pacific Ocean off the Chilean coast between 33° and 40° south latitude.

Irrawaddy River Dolphin *Orcaella brevirostris*   Plate 22

Other Name: Irrawaddy Dolphin.
Length: 7 feet (2.1 meters).
Weight: 220 pounds (100 kilograms).
Description: A dark-gray dolphin with an unusual round head and a low dorsal ridge on which is placed a small dorsal fin.
Food: Fish.
Habitat: Coastal waters, estuaries, and muddy river entrances where strong tidal currents occur.
Distribution: The Indian Ocean and South China Sea from North Borneo to the Bay of Bengal; also ventures up the Irrawaddy, Ganges, and Mekong Rivers.

Northern Right Whale Dolphin *Lissodelphis borealis* Plate 21

Other Name: Peale's Dolphin.
Length: 8 feet (2.4 meters).
Weight: 180 pounds (82 kilograms).
Description: An attractive, slim, grayish-black dolphin with white undersides. There is no dorsal fin.
Food: Fish and squid.
Habitat: Deep, cold ocean waters.
Distribution: The eastern Pacific Ocean from the Bering Sea south to California (San Diego); the western north Pacific Ocean from the Bering Sea south to Japan.

Southern Right Whale Dolphin *Lissodelphis peronii*   Plate 21

Other Name: Peron's Dolphin.
Length: 6 feet (1.8 meters).
Weight: 150 pounds (68 kilograms).
Description: An unusually attractive species, dark above and white on the face, sides, flippers, flukes, and undersides. There is no dorsal fin.
Food: Fish and squid.
Habitat: Deep oceanic waters.
Distribution: Waters surrounding South America from southern Brazil and Argentina to the south Atlantic Ocean around the Horn to Chile (37° south latitude) in the south Pacific Ocean; waters around New Zealand and Tasmania to New Guinea; Atlantic Ocean waters off South Africa; and Antarctic Ocean waters.

Phocoenidae: Porpoises

The species included here are small animals with blunt heads. They prefer coastal waters, although some venture farther to sea.

Harbor Porpoise *Phocoena phocoena*   Plate 23

Other Names: Common Porpoise, Puffing Pig, Herring Hog.
Length: 5 feet (1.5 meters).
Weight: 165 pounds (75 kilograms).
Description: A small, chunky, round-headed porpoise without a beak and with a dark brown or gray back, grayish-brown sides, and white below extending onto the sides ahead of the small, triangular dorsal fin. A narrow black line extends from the mouth to the base of the flippers. The flippers are dark. It is very difficult to approach and is reported in numbers ranging from 2 to about 100, but most often from 5 to 10.
Food: Fish, shrimp, and squid.
Habitat: Shallow coastal waters less than 100 fathoms, harbors, bays, and occasionally up rivers.
Distribution: In the eastern Arctic and north Atlantic Oceans from Barents Sea, Iceland, and the Davis Strait south to the Black Sea, Azov Sea, and Mediterranean Sea and the Senegal coast; in the western north Atlantic Ocean south to Delaware. In the western north Pacific Ocean from the Arctic south to Japan; in the eastern north Pacific Ocean from Alaska (Point Barrow) south to Mexico (Jaliso).

Spectacled Porpoise *Phocoena dioptrica*   Plate 24

Other Names: None.
Length: 5 feet (1.5 meters).
Weight: 120 pounds (54 kilograms).
Description: A beautiful black-and-white porpoise that may or may not have a dark line between the mouth and flippers. The animals black, triangular-shaped dorsal fin is absent in the somewhat similarly colored Southern Right Whale Dolphin.
Food: Fish.
Habitat: Cold waters inshore.
Distribution: The south Atlantic from Rio de La Plata (Argentina) south to Tierra del Fuego, the Falkland Islands, and South Georgia. Possibly also the south Pacific along coastal Chile south of 36° south latitude.

Black Porpoise *Phocoena spinipinnis*   Plate 23

Other Name: Burmeister Porpoise.

Length: 5 feet (1.5 meters).

Weight: 120 pounds (54 kilograms).

Description: A black porpoise with an oddly shaped triangular dorsal fin.

Food: Fish.

Habitat: Cold inshore waters less than 10 fathoms deep.

Distribution: The eastern coast of South America from the mouth of the Rio da La Plata (Argentina) southward; also the western coast of South America from Paita, Peru (5° south latitude) southward.

Gulf of California Porpoise *Phocoena sinus*   Plate 23

Other Names: None.

Length: 5 feet (1.5 meters).

Weight: 110 pounds (50 kilograms).

Description: A lead-gray porpoise on the upper parts and white below. There is a triangular-shaped dorsal fin.

Food: Fish.

Habitat: Inhabits harbors and shallow coastal waters less than 10 fathoms deep.

Distribution: The north Pacific Ocean coastline from upper Gulf of California to the Tres Marías Islands and Banderas Bay (Jalisco, Mexico).

Black Finless Porpoise *Neophocaena phocaenoides*   Plate 23

Other Name: Finless Porpoise.

Length: 5 feet (1.5 meters).

Weight: 100 pounds (45 kilograms).

Description: A black or dark gray porpoise lacking a dorsal fin but with an obvious dorsal ridge.

Food: Fish, cuttlefish, and shrimp.

Habitat: Shallow waters, less than 10 fathoms deep, in estuaries.

Distribution: The Indian Ocean from the Bay of Bengal to South Africa; the south Pacific Ocean from the South China Sea and Chinese coast (and 1,000 miles or 1,600 kilometers inland in the Yangtze Kiang River as well as in Tungting Lake) to the southern coast of Japan.

Dall's Porpoise *Phocoenoides dalli*   Plate 24

Other Names: None.

Length: 6 feet (1.8 meters).

Weight: 300 pounds (136 kilograms).

Description: A black or dark grayish porpoise with a large white area on the flanks and white on the tip of the dorsal fin and flukes. There also are several white marks on the rear of the dark flippers. The True's Porpoise, showing extensive white areas on the sides, is considered a color phase found in waters around Japan.

Food: Squid and fish.

Habitat: Deep coastal and ocean waters, generally from 5 to 10 miles (8 to 16 kilometers) off coastlines, where water depths reach 100 to 1,000 fathoms.

Distribution: The western north Pacific Ocean from Siberia south to Japan; the eastern north Pacific Ocean from the Bering Sea south to northwestern Baja California.

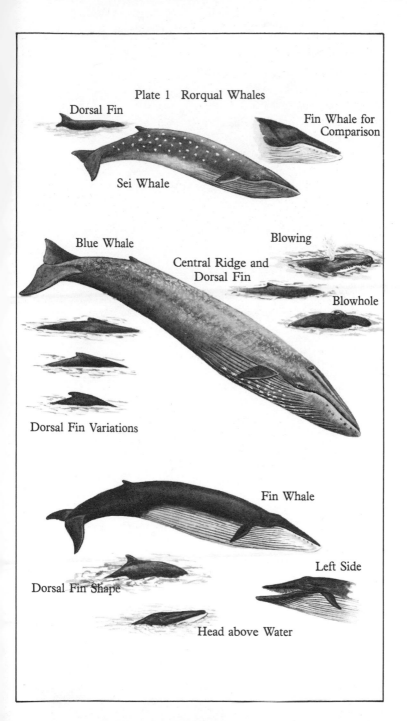

Plate 1 Rorqual Whales

Dorsal Fin

Fin Whale for Comparison

Sei Whale

Blue Whale

Blowing

Central Ridge and Dorsal Fin

Blowhole

Dorsal Fin Variations

Fin Whale

Dorsal Fin Shape

Left Side

Head above Water

Plate 2 Rorqual Whales

Minke Whale

Bryde's Whale

Humpback Whale

Humpback Female

Calf

Plate 3 Humpback Whale

Blowing Bubble Net

Breaching

Baleen Plates

Humpback Whale

Fluke Color Variations

Dorsal Fin Variations

Plate 4 Right Whales

Bowhead Whale

Bonnet and Baleen Plates

Black Right
Whale

Flukes During Dive

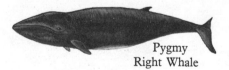

Pygmy
Right Whale

Plate 5 Gray Whale

Breaching

Spyhopping

Flukes in Dive

Gray Whale

Newly Born Calf

Plate 6   Beaked Whales

North Sea Beaked Whale

Strap-Toothed Whale

Gulf Stream Beaked Whale

True's Beaked Whale

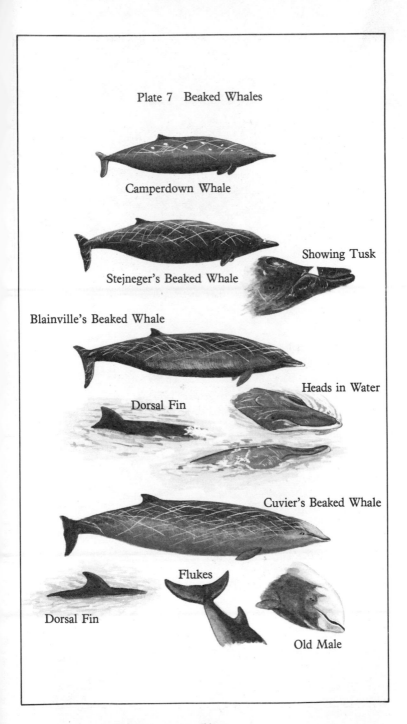

Plate 7 Beaked Whales

Camperdown Whale

Stejneger's Beaked Whale

Showing Tusk

Blainville's Beaked Whale

Dorsal Fin

Heads in Water

Cuvier's Beaked Whale

Dorsal Fin

Flukes

Old Male

Plate 8   Beaked Whales

Tasmanian Beaked Whale

Southern Beaked Whale

Baird's Beaked Whale

Plate 9 Beaked Whales

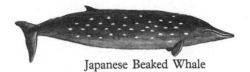

Japanese Beaked Whale

Hubb's Beaked Whale

Dorsal Fin
Variation

Old Male

Northern Bottlenose Whale

Plate 10 Sperm Whales

Dorsal Fin

Flukes

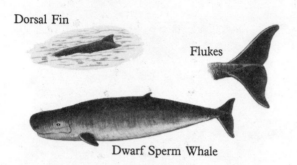

Dwarf Sperm Whale

Pygmy Sperm Whale

Flukes During Dive

Dorsal Fins

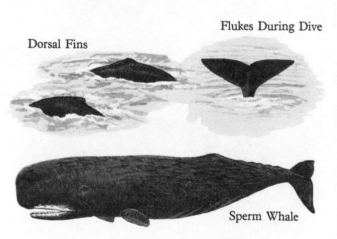

Sperm Whale

Plate 11 White Whales
Immature (center) and Adults under water

White Whale

Narwhal

Young Male

Male in Water

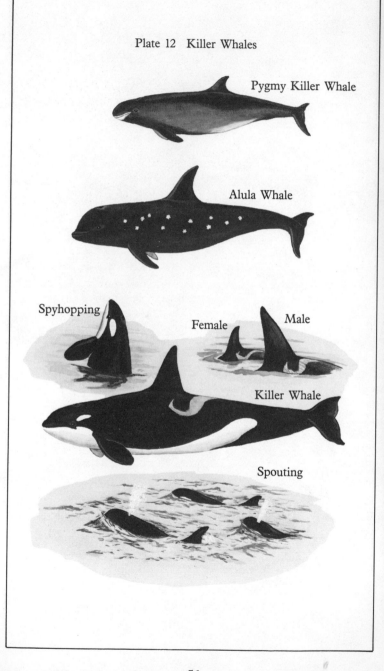

Plate 12   Killer Whales

Pygmy Killer Whale

Alula Whale

Spyhopping

Female   Male

Killer Whale

Spouting

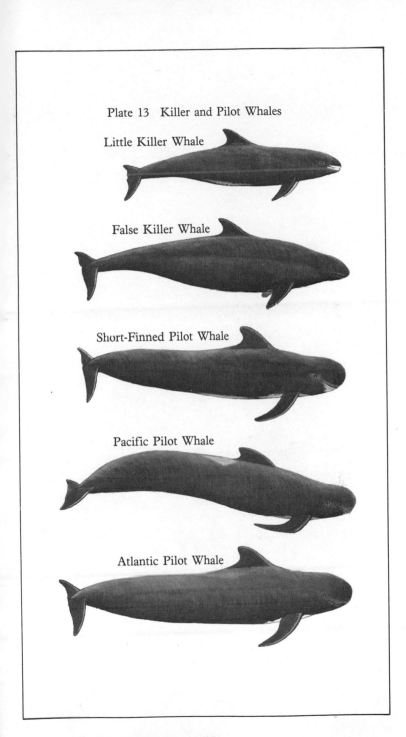

Plate 13 Killer and Pilot Whales

Little Killer Whale

False Killer Whale

Short-Finned Pilot Whale

Pacific Pilot Whale

Atlantic Pilot Whale

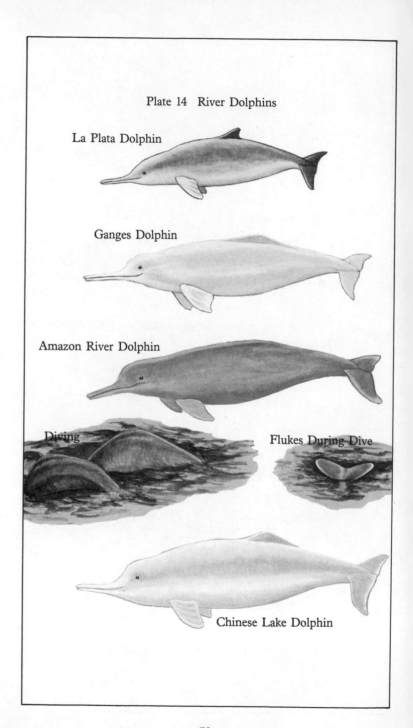

Plate 14 River Dolphins

La Plata Dolphin

Ganges Dolphin

Amazon River Dolphin

Diving

Flukes During Dive

Chinese Lake Dolphin

Plate 15   River Dolphins

Tucuxi Dolphin

Guiana River Dolphin

Cameroon Dolphin

Plate 16 Dolphins

Chinese White Dolphin

Speckled Dolphin

Plumbeous Dolphin

Blue Dolphin

Plate 17   Dolphins

Long-Beaked Dolphin

Bridled Dolphin

Atlantic Spotted Dolphin

Rough-Toothed Dolphin

Plate 18 Dolphins

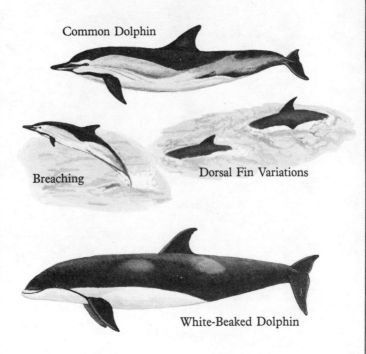

Narrow-Snouted Dolphin

Common Dolphin

Breaching

Dorsal Fin Variations

White-Beaked Dolphin

Plate 19 Dolphins

Hourglass Dolphin

Pacific White-Sided Dolphin

Atlantic White-Sided Dolphin

Sarawak Dolphin

Plate 20   Dolphins

Heaviside's Dolphin

White-Bellied Dolphin

Commerson's Dolphin

Hector's Dolphin

Hector's Dolphin (color variation)

Plate 21 Dolphins

Southern Right Whale Dolphin

Northern Right Whale Dolphin

Dusky Dolphin

Risso's Dolphin

Old Male

Plate 22 Dolphins

Irrawaddy River Dolphin

Bottlenosed Dolphin

Head

Diving

Plate 23 Porpoises

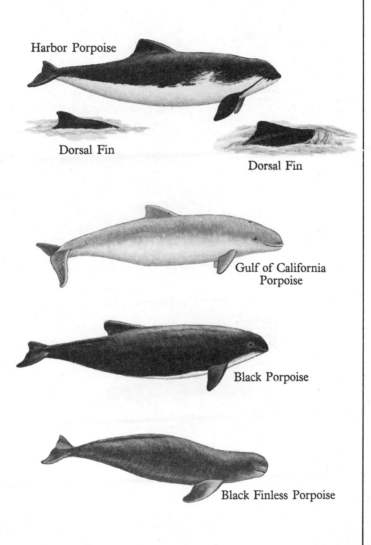

Harbor Porpoise

Dorsal Fin

Dorsal Fin

Gulf of California
Porpoise

Black Porpoise

Black Finless Porpoise

Plate 24   Porpoises

Spectacled Porpoise

Dall's Porpoise

Dall's Porpoise (color variation)

2
WHALE-WATCHING EQUIPMENT

The equipment used by recreational whale watchers to observe and study whales, dolphins, and porpoises is not unlike that used by bird watchers. Indeed, persons who observe albatrosses, shearwaters, petrels, and other pelagic birds also watch whales and other marine mammals just as eagerly as they do birds—and with exactly the same equipment for both activities. These items are the basic whale-watching tools.

Binoculars

A good pair of binoculars is essential for whale watching. Generally 7 × 35, 7 × 50, or 8 × 40 binoculars with coated lenses are used more frequently because they provide adequate magnification and a sufficiently wide field of view, allowing persons to detect and study whales, dolphins, and porpoises clearly. However, some observers use binoculars with slightly higher magnifications, such as 10X instruments, because they allow much more detail to be seen. Nevertheless, a person using 10X binoculars may find them somewhat difficult to hold steady, especially when he is standing on the deck of a moving ship.

In addition to magnification, the type of construction of binoculars is of critical consideration because they sometimes are accidentally exposed to salt spray which can seriously damage the instruments. Therefore, binoculars must either be well sealed against outside elements or encased in rubber to provide complete waterproofing. The latter obviously are less likely to suffer external or internal damage because of exposure to water. Most major binoculars manufacturers sell sealed roof prism models which are excellent. Carl Zeiss and a few other companies also have rubber-encased models. The most expensive of these are superb optical instruments which will last a lifetime if they are used properly. Therefore, when buying binoculars, do not pinch pennies; buy the very best that you can afford.

Telescopes

Telescopes, such as those used by bird watchers, also are extremely useful to whale watchers stationed on land lookouts or observatories overlooking seacoasts, bays, and lagoons. Generally 20X or 30X magnifications are selected, but sometimes much higher magnifications are desirable. Such instruments should have coated lenses and be mounted on heavy photographic tripods to provide a steady base of support. Use of telescopes on board ships is less useful because the ship's movement is magnified greatly; it also is difficult to hold the scopes steady. However, a wooden gunstock sometimes can be successfully used as a support for such telescopes. Bird watchers commonly use this technique.

Cameras

Many whale watchers also enjoy taking photographs of these splendid creatures and consider a good camera an essential part of their whale-watching equipment.

A single-lens, reflex-type 35mm camera equipped with a 400mm telephoto lens is ideal. Both lens and camera should be mounted onto a wooden gunstock or other shoulder support for easy operation. Cameras with shutter speeds up to $\frac{1}{1,000}$th second are preferable because one must be able to stop ship, whale, and photographer motion. Therefore, take most photographs at a shutter speed of $\frac{1}{1,000}$th second whenever possible.

Occasionally, whales can be approached within a few feet or even touched at certain calving lagoons and bays. Under those circumstances a camera's normal lens (usually 50mm focal length) can be used. However, close approach to these animals is not recommended because of the disturbance inflicted upon the whales and various changes in their behavior that sometimes result from very close encounters with people and boats.

Therefore, long telephoto lenses are much preferred when one wishes to take good photographs. Their use frequently permits photos to be taken from safe distances with little or no impact upon the whales or their behavior. Indeed, it should go without saying—but nevertheless can't be stressed too strongly—that the welfare of the whales (or dolphins or porpoises) always must receive first consideration, even if that means not taking photographs. To see and perhaps photograph whales and other marine mammals is a privilege that should never be abused.

Recordings

A variety of commercial recordings of the sounds of Humpback Whales and a few other species are now available at modest cost. Every whale watcher will want to purchase copies of these records and listen to the hauntingly beautiful voices of these magnificent mammals. In addition to commercial recordings, the National Geographic Society included in its January 1979 issue of *National Geographic* magazine a splendid record entitled "Songs of the Humpback Whale" with commentary by Dr. Roger Payne.

Following are the names of whale and dolphin recordings and the companies which produced and released them. Available in record stores, they also are available from General Whale, P. O. Box Whales, Alameda, California 94501 or from the Whale Protection Fund, 2100 M. Street, N. W., Washington, D. C. 20037.

Record Title	Producer
Songs of the Humpback Whale	Capitol Records
Deep Voices	Capitol Records
Sounds and Ultrasounds of the Bottle-Nose Dolphin	Folkways Records

Clothing

Depending upon where you engage in whale watching, special types of clothing may be required. As a general rule of thumb, air temperatures tend to be much cooler on board boats and ships at sea; whale watchers should always carry warm clothing such as parkas, heavy sweaters, and gloves. A hat is equally necessary, both for protection from the sun and (in cold climates) for warmth. In some instances, foul-weather clothing or other waterproof clothing may be needed. Even if one watches whales from land lookouts or observatories, some of these items will be useful or necessary, depending upon where the observatory is located.

Other items

In addition to clothing, many other items are also helpful to the recreational whale watcher. Sunglasses, for example, always help reduce glare from the surface of water, and suntan lotion is necessary in tropical climates. The whale watcher should also carry along a small notebook and pencil so that details of whale-watching efforts can be recorded for future reference, e.g., date, location, species, numbers of whales observed, and notes on behavior. Even rough field sketches of patterns of body markings and spout patterns are useful. Indeed, the more information and drawings recorded in a whale-watching notebook, the more valuable and useful the notebook becomes.

Whale sighting report forms

The use of printed whale sighting report forms (see appendix) offers observers a particularly effective and convenient way to gather and record information on whale sightings. Since the forms are preprinted and require specific information, whale watchers can't overlook or forget to note all of the essential information for a sighting. Field data forms, or report forms, are already used widely in many other branches of wildlife biology and their value is solidly established. Whale watchers who do not already use report forms also can benefit from their use.

3
WATCHING AND IDENTIFYING WHALES, DOLPHINS, AND PORPOISES

Most people are unfamiliar with the species of whales, dolphins, and porpoises because they have opportunities to see these marine mammals only rarely, such as an occasional ocean cruise, deep-sea fishing trip, or pelagic bird-watching trip. Therefore, people generally find that the correct identification of these animals is very difficult, sometimes impossible. In fact, whale watchers never should expect to identify all their sightings correctly, nor should they hesitate to list some animals observed as unidentified. When in doubt about the identity of marine mammals, admit that doubt.

Levels of identification

Three levels of identification can be applied to sightings of whales, dolphins, and porpoises. The level achieved on a particular sighting depends upon various factors, including how well the animal is seen, if major field marks are observed, the skill of the observer, and the experience of the observer. Even the equipment used by the observer will influence his ability, or lack of ability, to identify his sightings correctly. In more cases than not, however, be cautious when trying to identify marine mammals.

Observers should not be disappointed when they can't identify all the animals they see. In many instances, however, it is possible to recognize whales and other cetaceans as belonging to a particular group or family (such as rorqual whales or beaked whales) but not to a specific species. Under those circumstances, whale watchers often add speculative notations to their notes on such sightings, such as

73

"rorqual whale—probably a Sei Whale" or whichever species they suspect the animal to be. Such speculation is justified as long as it is noted.

The third level of identification involves certain recognition of a whale, dolphin, or porpoise to actual species. Thus, one actually notes a sighting as a Humpback Whale, Killer Whale, Bottlenosed Dolphin, Harbor Porpoise, etc. Specific recognition of whales and other cetaceans is the most useful and desirable level of identification to achieve, but it is also the most difficult.

Geographic distribution

The known geographic distribution of the species of whales, dolphins, and porpoises is a particularly helpful tool when attempting to identify these animals. Some species range widely in the oceans of the world, but other species have ranges that apparently are extremely restricted. Thus, by a process of elimination, based upon the known geographic distribution of the various species, the most likely species to occur in your area can be considered first. In many cases, this elimination process will lead you to the correct identification of the species observed. If not, then more unlikely possibilities must be considered.

For example, if you observe migrating whales off the coastline of California, it is likely that they are Gray Whales. First turn to the description and illustration plate for that species to determine if the animals are, in fact, Gray Whales. If not, then other somewhat less likely possibilities must be considered and the process repeated until some level of identification is achieved. It is important to remember, however, that the geographic distributions of many species of whales are known imperfectly; a species not indigenous to a particular area may appear there anyway.

Seasonal distribution

Whale watchers also should consider the seasonal distribution of the various species as they attempt to identify the animals they observe. Many species are highly migratory. They engage in long-distance travels extending for thousands of miles or kilometers of ocean in order to arrive at wintering areas far removed from breeding and/or calving areas. Thus, the season during which a whale is seen provides another helpful clue to the identity of the animal. Nevertheless, it is always possible to see a given species in an area during a period when that species normally does not occur there. Sick or injured animals sometimes linger behind and may account for such out-of-season sightings.

Rareness

The rareness of a given species of whale or other cetacean is another factor to consider when making an identification of a sighting. While it is still possible to observe some endangered species, the fact that these species are now so rare makes such sightings less likely than sightings of whales or other cetaceans that still survive in larger numbers. However, when an engangered species such as a Blue Whale is actually observed (as individuals are from time to time), the event is very special for recreational whale watchers.

Spout patterns

The spout patterns of the various larger species of whales are also very helpful clues to the identity of some whales. The spout patterns of seven large species are shown here for comparison.

Diving patterns

The way various large whales hold their bodies when they dive is yet another helpful clue to the correct identification of some of these species. Particularly important is the shape of the animal's back and the position of the flukes as the whale goes underwater. Combinations of these field marks for seven large whale species are shown for comparison.

Spyhopping

Occasionally, Gray Whales and various other species surface and push their large heads vertically out of the water for up to 30 seconds in what is termed spyhopping, the spy-out, or spar position. When they do this, whale watchers enjoy superb views of the heads of the huge animals. This behavior is not fully understood, but it may simply be the whales trying to look around. It has also been suggested that spyhopping may be courtship behavior or that it may aid the whales in swallowing food.

Plate 25   Whale Diving and Spouting Patterns

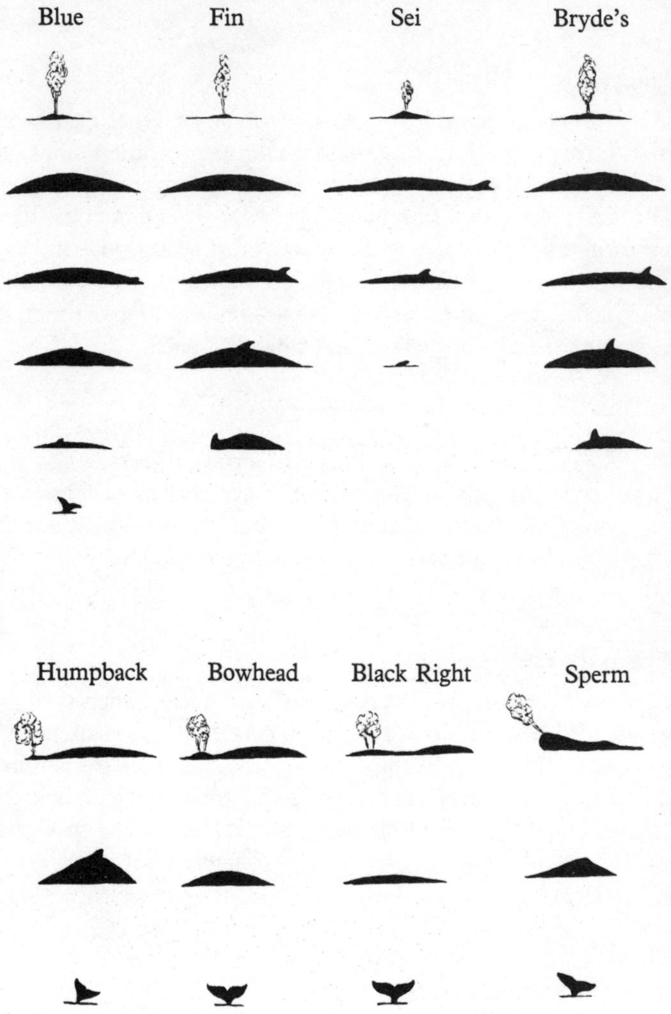

Blue   Fin   Sei   Bryde's

Humpback   Bowhead   Black Right   Sperm

Breaching

From time to time, solitary Gray Whales and other species leap above the waterline at roughly a 45° angle then fall back into the water, accompanied by a huge splash. On rare occasions this breaching may occur as frequently as 25 times within an hour.

The reason why whales breach is unknown, but some evidence suggests that unusual sounds, including low-flying airplanes, may be related to this behavior. Some scientists also speculate that whales breach in order to remove whale lice from their skins.

Regardless of the reason for the behavior, a breaching whale is a spectacular sight that will not soon be forgotten. However, it happens so quickly that many whale watchers miss the breach unless they are constantly alert.

Atlantic Pilot Whales spyhopping (photo by Jeffrey Goodyear)

Humpback Whale breaching (photo by Jeffrey Goodyear).

Body markings

Various whale species also have different body markings, as is obvious from an inspection of the identification plates in this guide. In some, the field marks are subtle; in others the body markings are distinctive and serve as excellent aids to identification. Therefore, particular attention should be given to the body markings of whales and other cetaceans.

In addition to more or less general body markings for a given species, there is also considerable variation among individuals of some species of whales. For example, the fluke patterns of Humpback Whales vary enormously and are unique to each individual, much like human fingerprints are unique to each person. Therefore, it is possible to recognize individual Humpback Whales based upon the markings on the flukes.

In a similar manner, the body markings on Killer Whales vary, as they do on many other species. Still, the variation in individual whale body markings is not so great that the general pattern for the species is lost.

Dorsal fin and body size

The presence or absence of a dorsal fin on a whale is an extremely quick and helpful clue to identifying some whale species. Generally, whale watchers do not have opportunities to see the entire animal and all of its field marks in the water. However, one usually sees the back of a whale and can look carefully for the presence of a dorsal fin. Thus, if a fin is not present, the animal is not one of the rorqual whales or the beaked whales. However, it might be one of the right whales or a Gray Whale.

On the other hand, if one sees a whale in the water and it has a dorsal fin, note the size, shape, and approximate location of the fin on the animal's back. For example, the dorsal fins of rorqual whales are distinct, whereas the dorsal fins on beaked whales are less distinct and are placed far back toward the flukes. In some cases, such as the Killer Whale, the dorsal fin of the adult male is larger and shaped differently than that of adult females and young animals. The size and shape of the dorsal fin on Humpback Whales, however, exhibit considerable variation. Thus, paying close attention to a whale's dorsal fin is enormously helpful in correctly identifying a whale.

The body size (length) of any cetacean observed in the water, when considered in combination with the presence or absence of a dorsal fin, can also serve as a quick and helpful clue to the animal's identity. For example, cetaceans of the western north Atlantic Ocean can be separated into three basic body size (length) groups: large (40 to 85 feet; 12 to 26 meters), medium (13 to 32 feet; 4 to 10 meters); and small (less than 13 feet; 4 meters).

The following chart, adapted from Leatherwood, Caldwell, and Winn's *Whales, Dolphins, and Porpoises of the Western North Atlantic,* summarizes the body size (length) and dorsal fin combinations of the cetaceans of these waters.

Size–Dorsal Fin Characters
Western North Atlantic Cetaceans

Body size (length)	With dorsal fin	Without dorsal fin
Large	Blue Whale	
Large	Fin Whale	
Large	Sei Whale	
Large	Bryde's Whale	
Large	Humpback Whale	
Large		Bowhead Whale
Large		Black Right Whale
Large		Sperm Whale
Medium	Minke Whale	
Medium	Northern Bottlenose Whale	
Medium	Cuvier's Beaked Whale	
Medium	All other beaked whales	
Medium	Killer Whale	
Medium	False Killer Whale	
Medium	Atlantic Pilot Whale	
Medium	Short-Finned Pilot Whale	
Medium		White Whale
Medium		Narwhal
Small	Atlantic Spotted Dolphin	
Small	Long-Beaked Dolphin	
Small	Blue Dolphin	

Body size (length)	With dorsal fin	Without dorsal fin
Small	Common Dolphin	
Small	Sarawak Dolphin	
Small	Atlantic White-Sided Dolphin	
Small	White-Beaked Dolphin	
Small	Bottlenosed Dolphin	
Small	Guiana River Dolphin	
Small	Rough-Toothed Dolphin	
Small	Pygmy Killer Whale	
Small	Little Killer	
Small	Pygmy Sperm Whale	
Small	Dwarf Sperm Whale	
Small	Harbor Porpoise	

In the following table, the dorsal fin-body size (length) combinations of the cetaceans of the eastern north Pacific Ocean are also summarized, based upon information presented by Leatherwood, Evans, and Rice in *The Whales, Dolphins, and Porpoises of the Eastern North Pacific.*

Size–Dorsal Fin Characters
Eastern North Pacific Cetaceans

Body size (length)	With dorsal fin	Without dorsal fin
Large	Blue Whale	
Large	Fin Whale	
Large	Humpback Whale	
Large		Black Right Whale
Large		Gray Whale
Large		Sperm Whale
Medium	Minke Whale	
Medium	Beaked Whales	
Medium	Killer Whale	
Medium	Pacific Pilot Whale	
Medium	Risso's Dolphin	
Small	Common Dolphin	

Body size (length)	With dorsal fin	Without dorsal fin
Small	Pacific White-Sided Dolphin	
Small	Bottlenosed Dolphin	
Small	Harbor Porpoise	
Small	Dall's Porpoise	
Small		Northern Right Whale Dolphin

Shore lookouts or observatories

In various parts of the world, often on cliffs or headlands overlooking the sea, it is possible to observe migrating whales at the proper seasons of the year. Such land observatories are superb ways to see these marine mammals without any danger of distrubing them. Indeed, the use of shore lookouts or observatories is to be encouraged whenever possible over the popular (but unwise) use of boats to observe whales. One shore observatory for whale watching is maintained by the National Park Service at Cabrillo National Monument near San Diego, California. Not only are formal facilities available there for this activity, but trained rangers present 15-20 minute auditorium programs during the whale migration months. Included in the programs is a motion picture about the California Gray Whale. Rangers also are present at the whale observatory to assist visitors in finding the large mammals as they swim past the site. Similar formal whale-watching programs are also provided at some of the other whale lookouts or observatories.

Whale strandings

Almost anyone who reads newspapers sees photographs of whales that become stranded on beaches or coastlines from time to time. The reasons for such strandings are still imperfectly understood, but they provide interested whale watchers and other persons with superb opportunities to observe these cetaceans (often dead) at close range and observe the important field marks of the species clearly and at leisure. While the small and medium-sized species are often found, even large whales occasionally are stranded. For example, in 1979 an 85-foot Blue Whale was found dead on a California beach; that same year numerous Sperm Whales were stranded on an Oregon beach. Some examples of other species of whales that be-

come stranded on beaches include Fin, Black Right, Killer, and
False Killer Whales. Occasionally, various species of dolphins and
porpoises also become stranded.

Scientists with special interests in whales are also very interested in stranded whales and other cetaceans because they can
secure much important information from careful study of the specimens. Therefore, when such strandings are discovered, they should
be reported immediately to the nearest office of the National Marine Fisheries Services (see appendix) or to any large natural history museum.

Sperm Whales stranded on an Oregon beach (photo by James R. Larison,
Oregon State University Sea Grant College Program).

Oceanaria and zoos

Still another place in which the smaller species of whales, dolphins, and porpoises may be observed alive is in oceanaria and zoos in various parts of the world. Generally, the more common species are exhibited, but occasionally even Killer Whales are placed on display or included in various trained acts. However, none of the so-called great whales such as the Sperm Whale is exhibited in oceanaria or zoos, and it is very unlikely that they ever will be—they are simply too large to handle. To see them, one must venture onto the oceans, sometimes in remote places, then be satisfied with brief views of the animals. Nevertheless, visits to oceanaria and zoos are worthwhile and provide fine opportunities to observe some of the smaller and more common cetaceans.

Exhibits

Prior to participating in recreational whale watching, a visit to a major natural history museum or a museum with a special interest in cetaceans can be an educational experience. Such museums have exhibits dealing with whales and other cetaceans, and one can learn a good deal about these marine mammals and their lives from careful examination and study of such exhibits. In a similar manner The Whale Center's whale bus takes exhibits to schools and other places in the Oakland, California, area where large numbers of people gather.

Whale festivals

Whale festivals, such as those held each year on National Environmental Day by the Cabrillo Marine Museum in cooperation with the American Cetacean Society, provide excellent educational opportunities to teach children and other interested persons about cetaceans and the need to preserve, protect, and conserve these marine mammals. The festival is held on Cabrillo Beach, San Pedro, California, where more than 1,000 children and adults—all community volunteers—construct life-size Blue and Gray Whales and calves in the sand. Such efforts call to public attention the struggle for survival that whales face. Thus, whale festivals serve as excellent public relations tools to be used with skill and imagination to foster better public appreciation and concern for whales (and other cetaceans) and their survival.

A male Killer Whale on exhibit at Sea World in California. (photo courtesy of Sea World).

Cabrillo Marine Museum's whale festival featuring a sand whale constructed on a beach (photo courtesy of Los Angeles Recreation and Park Department).

Safety and whale watching

Experienced whale watchers never forget that caution is always in order when looking at cetaceans from boats or ships or from land sites. Not infrequently, such as in the Gulf of Maine, strong and dangerous currents and tides and fog or other unexpected weather conditions can create dangerous—even fatal—conditions for inexperienced persons. Thus inexperienced persons should never use small boats in unfamiliar waters for whale watching. If one must go to sea to watch whales, join other persons on a charter vessel operated by an experienced captain and crew in waters they know well.

Land lookouts, of course, are generally much safer than pelagic trips, but great caution must be taken even at many land sites, especially at places where tides can quickly isolate persons from safety on high ground. Thus, concern for safety always must temper a whale watcher's enthusiasm and desire to take foolish risks. When visiting an area with strong, high tides, check local tide tables carefully before leaving places of safety and return to safe, high ground before tides begin rushing in.

4
WHALE MIGRATIONS

The migrations of whales are legendary. It is worthwhile, therefore, to discuss several of the better-known examples of these marine mammal movements such as those of the Gray Whale, Humpback Whale, Killer Whale, and rorqual whales of the southern hemisphere.

Gray Whale

The migrations of the Gray Whales (or California Gray Whales) that inhabit the eastern north Pacific Ocean from Alaska southward to the Bay of California are famous and extremely popular wildlife attractions each year to hundreds of thousands of interested and concerned people. These migrations probably are known as well as any whale migrations anywhere in the world.

California Gray Whales spend their summers (roughly April to September) in the Arctic Ocean surrounding Alaska. At about the end of September, they begin migrating southward by crossing the Bering Sea and entering the north Pacific Ocean. The animals then follow the coastline, sometimes just off the kelp beds, of western North America southward. They move at a rate of about 100 miles per day. By January, they arrive in several shallow lagoons along the coast of Baja California in Mexico. There they give birth to their calves and spend the rest of the winter. By late February the females and calves leave the Baja California lagoons, head into the Pacific Ocean, and slowly move northward (following poorly known routes) until they arrive again in summer in the waters off Alaska including the Arctic Ocean and waters off Siberia. Thus, the migrations of California Gray Whales extend over 8,000 miles and are among the longest migrations of any animals known.

Gray Whale migration routes. Redrawn after Leatherwood, Evans, and Rice (1972).

Humpback Whale

The various populations of the Humpback Whale are also extremely fascinating, and their behavior and migrations have been studied intensively in recent years. Thus, the basics of their migration patterns are known.

In the north Atlantic Ocean, for example, Humpbacks migrate from Bermuda to southern Greenland and northeastern Canada; in European waters they move from the Arctic southward to waters off northwestern Africa. Still other Humpbacks migrate from waters off Southern Africa south to cold Antarctic waters.

In the Indian Ocean, the whales migrate from Madagascar southward to the Antarctic.

Both sides of northern South America also witness Humpback Whale migrations south to Antarctic waters off the western side of the Antarctic Peninsula. There also are migrations in the north Pacific Ocean, especially from the waters surrounding the Hawaiian Islands to Alaska and the west coast of Canada and the United States. Still other migrations occur between the Fiji Islands and New Zealand and between Australia and Antarctica.

Thus, Humpback Whales roam all the world's oceans. In summer they feed in cold waters; in winter they calve in warmer tropical waters.

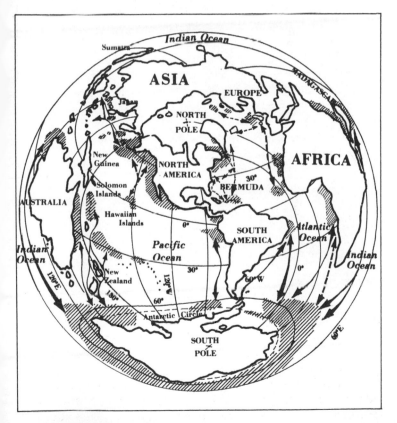

Humpback Whale migration routes.

Other whale migrations

In addition to the migrations of Gray and Humpback Whales, other species also engage in migrations that are less well-known but nevertheless interesting. For example, some rare Greenland Right Whales apparently migrate across the Greenland Sea from the northwestern end of Spitsbergen southwestward to the southeastern coast of Greenland, then back again. Other individuals of the same species, however, migrate from the Barents Sea westward past Jan Mayen Island to coastal Greenland and back again.

Fin Whales, on the other hand, use a variety of migration routes to various parts of the world. Some individuals move northward from Antarctic waters into the Indian Ocean; others migrate northward past eastern New Zealand; still others migrate northward to Cape Horn, then along the coast of Chile. Yet other Fin Whales seem to migrate between South Georgia and coastal South America south of Rio de Janeiro. Still more members of the species move northward to the Cape of Good Hope region. And, finally, some Fin Whales migrate north from Antarctic waters past Gough Island to an area in the central south Atlantic Ocean west of St. Helena.

Where the migrations of many other species of whales take them remains a mystery yet to be explored by scientists and explorers. Hopefully each of the species will survive so that, in time, we may yet enjoy a more perfect understanding and appreciation of these splendid marine mammals.

5
WHALE-WATCHING LOOKOUTS AND SANCTUARIES

In addition to the unexpected observation of whales and other cetaceans from the decks of ships sailing on the oceans and seas of the world, it is also possible to observe whales from certain islands, headlands, cliffs, bluffs, and shorelines of bays and inlets in various parts of the world. The whale-watching lookouts and sanctuaries listed here sometimes produce views of whales at the season(s) of the year indicated. However, the presence of whales at many of the sites tends to be unpredictable, and whale watchers should never develop unreasonably high expectations when visiting any of the locations. Frequently, repeated visits coupled with long hours of careful observation are required before brief views of whales are enjoyed. Nevertheless, persons seriously interested in seeing whales will find their efforts eventually rewarded.

Argentina

Peninsula Valdes
Whales: Black Right.
Viewing Season: May to December.
Description: Twin bays, one along each site of Peninsula Valdes, about halfway down the Argentine coast in northern Patagonia. Whale watching is possible from elevated shore points as the whales play, feed, and calve close to shore.

Access: Remote and difficult to reach except via special trek or expedition. Occasionally, however, commercial nature tours visit the area. Such tours are sometimes listed in national wildlife and conservation magazines.

Address: None.

The relative location of Peninsula Valdes, Argentina.

Bermuda

The waters around Bermuda are important breeding areas for Humpback Whales during several months of the year, and headlands along the island's South Shore can be used for whale watching. In addition to Humpbacks, Pilot Whales and Cuvier's Beaked Whales also occur in Bermuda's waters but are difficult, if not impossible, to see from land. The following land sites—marked on most Bermuda tourist maps—can be used for whale watching.

Church Bay (in Southampton Parish)
Whales: Humpback, Pilot.
Viewing Season: April (February to May) for Humpback; April and May for Pilot.
Description: Headlands overlooking Church Bay on the island's southern shore.
Access: Via South Road to the vicinity of the bay.
Address: Conservation Officer, Bermuda Department of Agriculture and Fisheries, P. O. Box 834, Hamilton 5, Bermuda.

Gibbs Hill Lighthouse (in Southampton Parish)
Whales: Humpback, Pilot.
Viewing Season: April (February to May) for Humpback; April and May for Pilot.
Description: A lighthouse hill overlooking the South Shore or headlands nearby overlooking the South Shore.
Access: Via South Road to Lighthouse Road, then Lighthouse Road north to Gibbs Hill Lighthouse.
Address: Conservation Officer, Bermuda Department of Agriculture and Fisheries, P. O. Box 834, Hamilton 5, Bermuda.

Spittal Pond National Park (in Smith's Parish)
Whales: Humpback, Pilot.
Viewing Season: April (February to May) for Humpback; April and May for Pilot.
Description: Headlands or other high areas overlooking the southern shore.
Access: Via South Road to the park and its vicinity.
Access: Conservation Officer, Bermuda Department of Agriculture and Fisheries, P. O. Box 834, Hamilton 5, Bermuda.

St. David's Head (in St. George's Parish)
Whales: Humpback, Pilot.
Viewing Season: April (February to May) for Humpback; April and May for Pilot.
Description: Headlands near the southeastern end of the island from which whales can be seen in inshore waters.
Access: Via Great Bay Road to Battery Road, then via Battery

Road to its end near St. David's Head.

Address: Conservation Officer, Bermuda Department of Agriculture and Fisheries, P. O. Box 834, Hamilton 5, Bermuda.

Canada

British Columbia

Vancouver Island (near Tofino)

Whales: Gray, Humpback, and Killer.

Viewing Season: March and April.

Description: Cliffs, bluffs, headlands, and other elevated sites along the west coast of Vancouver Island, including Pacific Rim National Park, from which whales can be observed in the coastal waters. A small population of Gray Whales resides along the island's west coast.

Access: From Port Alberni on Vancouver Island, drive west on Route 4 to the town of Ucluelet, then north along the island's west coast to Tofino. En route watch for whales from suitable pull-overs or other observation sites along the highway.

Address: None.

New Brunswick

Campobello Island (near Lubec, Maine)

Whales: Pilot, Fin, Humpback, and Black Right.

Viewing Season: April through November.

Description: Exposed views of coastal waters as seen from Head Harbor Light.

Access: From Lubec, Maine, drive a short distance east on State Route 189, cross a bridge and the international border and continue onto Campobello Island where local directions to Head Harbor Light can be secured.

Address: None.

Grand Manan Island (off Lubec, Maine)

Whales: Pilot, Fin, Humpback, and Black Right.

Viewing Season: April through November.

Description: Exposed views of coastal waters as seen from cliffs, headlands, and other spots along the island's shoreline.

Access: Via ferry from St. Andrews, New Brunswick.

Address: None.

Machias Seal Island (off Cutler, Maine)

Whales: Pilot, Fin, Humpback, and Black Right.

Viewing Season: April through November.

Description: A small rock-bordered island in the Gulf of Maine from which it is occasionally possible to observe whales in surrounding waters. A lighthouse and support buildings are constructed on the island. Overnight accommodations may be possible at the convenience of the lighthouse keepers.

Access: Formerly via fishing boats from Cutler, Maine. Now access is difficult, but it may be possible to arrange visits to the island either in Cutler or in nearby fishing villages along the Maine coast.

A Humpback Whale diving in Bonavista Bay, Newfoundland. (photo by Jeffrey Goodyear).

Newfoundland

Bonavista

Whales: Humpback.

Viewing Season: June through August.

Description: The shoreline of Cape Bonavista from which whales can be seen in adjacent waters.

Access: From Clarenville drive north on Provincial Route 10 for many miles to its junction with Provincial Route 24 near Summerville. Then continue north on Provincial Route 24 to the town of Bonavista near the tip of Cape Bonavista. Inquire

in the town for suitable whale-watching spots or look for
cetaceans from the coastline overlooking Bonavista Bay and
nearby waters.

Address: None.

Cape Race

Whales: Humpback.

Viewing Season: June through August.

Description: The shoreline in the vicinity of Cape Race from which
whales appear in adjacent waters.

Access: From St. John's drive south for many miles on Provincial
Route 5 to the town of Cape Race at the southeastern end
of Newfoundland.

Address: None.

Cape St. John (near La Scie)

Whales: Humpback.

Viewing Season: June through August.

Description: The shoreline of Cape St. John, near the town of La
Scie, from which whales appear in adjacent waters.

Access: From the junction of Canadian Route 1 and Provincial
Route 72 southwest of Springdale, drive north on Provincial
Route 72 to its junction with Provincial Route 12 near Baie
Verte. The continue northeast on Provincial Route 12 to the
town of La Scie near the tip of Cape St. John. Inquire in the
town for additional local details on suitable whale-watching
sites along the coastline or explore the coastline and look for
whales in nearby waters.

Address: None.

Cape St. Mary's (near St. Brides)

Whales: Humpback.

Viewing Season: June through August.

Description: A high cliff and cove at the park headquarters building
from which whales are seen in waters at the base of the cliff.

Access: From the town of St. Brides, drive east on Highway 100 for
2.3 miles to a narrow, unpaved, unnumbered road leading right
(south) and follow it for another 8.4 miles to the St. Mary's
lighthouse and base of the cliffs. The park headquarters building is nearby. Park there. Park naturalists are available to
guide visitors to the best whale and bird-watching locations.

Address: Newfoundland Department of Tourism, Tourist Services

Division, Confederation Building, St. John's, Newfoundland, Canada.

Elliston
Whales: Humpback.
Viewing Season: June through August.
Description: The waters just offshore from Elliston, with observations possible from the town's coastline.
Access: From Clarenville, drive north on Provincial Route 10 for many miles to its junction with Provincial Route 24 near Summerville. Then continue north on Provincial Route 24 toward the town of Bonavista near the tip of Cape Bonavista. After passing through the town of Catalina, look for a road leading right (east) to Elliston and follow that road to the town.
Address: None.

A Humpback Whale breaching just offshore from Elliston, Newfoundland. (photo by Scott Kraus).

Notre Dame Bay
Whales: Humpback.
Viewing Season: June through August.
Description: A large bay in eastern Newfoundland in which whales appear. It may be possible occasionally to observe some of these marine mammals from the extensive coastline of the bay.
Access: No specific site can be provided, but various towns are located along the bay and provide access to its coastline. Among these towns are Little Bay, Robert's Arm, Leading Tickles South, Campbellton, Birchy Bay, and Summerford—all well marked on road maps of Newfoundland. A variety of provin-

cial roads leading off Canadian Route 1 provide access to these
    towns.
Address: None.

Renews
Whales: Humpback.
Viewing Season: June through August.
Description: The waters of a bay where the town of Renews is
    located.
Access: From St. John's, drive south on Provincial Route 5 for many
    miles to the town of Renews. Look for whales from the coast-
    line.
Address: None

St. Mary's Bay
Whales: Humpback.
Viewing Season: June through August.
Description: A large bay in southeastern Newfoundland in which
    whales appear in summer.
Access: No specific spot is available for whale watching, but various
    parts of the coastline in the vicinity of towns such as Branch,
    St. Mary's, St. Vincent's, and St. Shotts might be productive
    for whale watching. Consult a Newfoundland road map for di-
    rections to these towns.
Address: None.

Trinity Bay
Whales: Humpback, Killer.
Viewing Season: June through August.
Description: A very large bay in eastern Newfoundland in which
    whales sometimes appear and may perhaps be observed from
    parts of the coastline around the bay.
Access: A number of towns are located along Trinity Bay and can be
    reached from numerous provincial roads. Consult a road map
    of Newfoundland for directions to these towns.
Address: None.

Quebec
Forillon National Park (near Gaspé)
Whales: Humpback; perhaps other species as well.
Viewing Season: June through August.

Description: A lighthouse on a high cliff and rugged coastline on a
tiny peninsula overlooking the Atlantic Ocean. Whale watching is done from the base of the lighthouse or its immediate
vicinity.

Access: From the town of Gaspé on the Gaspé peninsula, drive north
on Highway 132 to Cap-aux-os, then continue about 1 mile
(1.6 kilometers) farther and follow a secondary road marked to
Grand Greve. Continue through Grand Greve to a dead-end
parking lot. Park there, cross a road barrier, and hike along the
steep lighthouse road to the lighthouse—about a 45-minute
hike. Watch for whales from the vicinity of the lighthouse.

Address: Superintendent, Forillon National Park, Box 1220, Gaspé,
Quebec, Canada GOC 1RO.

Riviere du Loup
Whales: White.
Viewing Season: July and August.
Description: The ferry dock extending into the St. Lawrence River.
White Whales occasionally are seen directly from the dock.
Access: In Riviere du Loup, drive to the ferry dock, park, and look
for whales from there.
Address: None.

St. Lawrence River Estuary (near Tadoussac)
Whales: Fin and White; Harbor Porpoise.
Viewing Season: July and August.
Description: The waters of the St. Lawrence River, especially in
the vicinity of the mouth of the Saguenay River near the town
of Tadoussac, or cliffs along the river down from Tadoussac.
Access: Via boat from Montreal or via automobile along Provincial
Route 138 northeast from Tadoussac to any cliffs with exposed
views over the nearby river in which whales appear.
Address: None.

Ecuador

Galapagos Islands National Park
Whales: Sei, Fin, Humpback, Cuvier's Beaked, Sperm, and Killer.
Viewing Season: Random observations. No particular viewing
season.

Description: The interior waters surrounding the Galapagos Islands. Sei Whales are seen off the northern end of Isabela Island. Humpback Whales are observed along the southern coast of Isabela Island. Killer Whales sometimes visit Academy Bay and the northeastern coast of Santa Cruz Island. Fin Whales occur in various locations. Cuvier's Beaked Whales occur also in various locations. Sperm Whales are reported on the equator between Galapagos and the South American mainland. **Note:** All whale sightings within Galapagos waters should be reported to the Director of the Charles Darwin Research Station on Santa Cruz Island, Galapagos.

Access: Usually via organized tours to Galapagos, then on board several tourist ships visiting the various major islands. Such cruises have professional park service guides and sometimes celebrated naturalists on board to assist visitors with wildlife observation and photography. Many such tours are listed in national conservation and wildlife magazines.

Address: Director, Charles Darwin Research Station, Isla Santa Cruz, Galapagos, Ecuador.

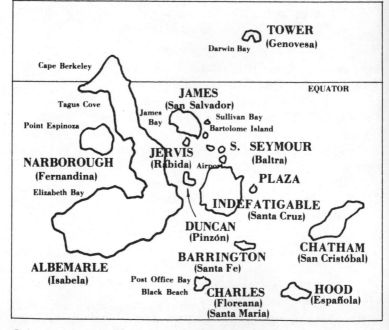

Galapagos Islands National Park, Ecuador.

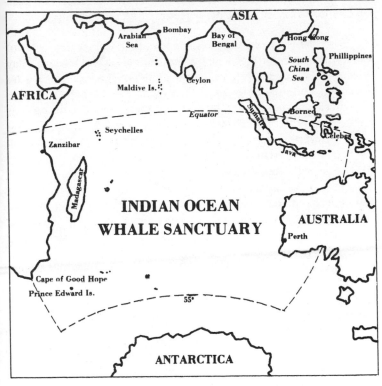

The Indian Ocean Whale Sanctuary.

Indian Ocean

Indian Ocean Whale Sanctuary

Whales: All whale species in Indian Ocean waters.

Viewing Season: All year, depending upon the species and location.

Description: A huge sanctuary consisting of the entire Indian Ocean north of 55° south latitude. The sanctuary was proposed by the government of the Seychelles and is solidly supported by conservationists throughout the world.

Access: Via ships sailing through the waters of the Indian Ocean.

Address: None.

Mexico

Along the isolated coast of portions of Baja California, in warm waters of several protected lagoons, and around several islands, Gray Whales spend several months on their calving grounds resting, reproducing, and providing care for their young until they grow large enough, strong enough, and fat enough to accompany their mothers northward to the summer feeding grounds in the Arctic.

It is clear, therefore, that the protection and preservation of these southern waters, islands, and lagoons is essential to the survival of Gray Whales in the eastern north Pacific Ocean. It also is clear that the whales must not be disturbed at this most important period each year. For this reason, the government of Mexico has designated the Baja California whale lagoons as whale refuges. It is now illegal for anyone without special permit to operate boats in these lagoons when the lagoons are inhabited by whales.

Despite these restrictions, however, it is possible to observe Gray Whales in the Baja California lagoons safely and without disturbing the mammals. Such observations can be made from land overlooking the lagoons.

Black Warrior Lagoon
Whales: Gray.
Viewing Season: Late December to early April.
Description: An abandoned dock formerly used for loading salt. Whales sometimes approach the dock at close range and provide excellent whale-watching opportunities.
Access: From Tijuana, drive south on Federal Highway 1 to the huge eagle statue beside the highway near the border between the Mexican states of Baja California and Terr Baja California. Continue southward on Highway 1, across the border, to the turn-off for the town of Guerrero Negro. Before reaching the main part of town, turn right at a stop sign near a supermarket owned by a company. Continue along this road for 7 miles (11.2 kilometers), passing salt marshes and estuaries, to the old dock.
Address: None.

San Lucas Area (extreme southern Terr Baja California)
Whales: Gray.

Viewing Season: January through March.

Description: Coastal waters as viewed from the area in front of the
Hotel Solmar or the balcony of the Hotel Finistierra. Whales
appear in nearby coastal waters.

Access: Via airplane to La Paz, then south via automobile on Federal
Highway 1 to San Jose del Cabo, then southwest on Route 9 to
the town of San Lucas.

Address: None.

Scammon's Lagoon

Whales: Gray.

Viewing Season: Late December to early April.

Description: An elevated area overlooking a major Gray Whale calving lagoon along the remote western coast of central Baja California in the state of Terr Baja California.

Access: Via Federal Highway 1 south from Tijuana. After driving 8
miles (12.8 kilometers) south past a huge eagle statue beside
the highway near the border between the Mexican states of Baja California and Terr Baja California, turn off at a signed
turn-off for Scammon's Lagoon (Laguna San Ignacio) and the
nearby salt flats and mining company, Exportadores de Sal.
Follow this unpaved road for 17 miles (27.2 kilometers) across
desert and around the southern end of the salt flats to its terminus at an elevated area (camping allowed for a nominal fee)
overlooking Scammon's Lagoon. Observe whales only from
the land overlooking the lagoon, not in boats in the lagoon.

Address: None.

Tijuana to Ensenada Toll Road

Whales: Gray.

Viewing Season: Late December to early April.

Description: A federal toll road which passes high overlooks where
whales can be observed in coastal waters.

Access: Easily, either at Tijuana on the Mexican-United States border or at Ensenada at the road's southern end. Look for especially productive whale-watching lookouts south of Ensenada
along a paved road leading to the town of La Bufadora.

Address: None.

South Georgia

Whales: Blue, Fin, Humpback, Black Right, Sperm, and Killer.
Other species also are observed at times.

Viewing Season: November to late January.

Description: A spectacular snow and ice-covered island located in
the Antarctic on the Scotia Ridge about 844 miles (1,350
kilometers) east-southeast of the Falkland Islands. It is located
in formerly extremely rich Antarctic whaling waters and still
provides visitors on board ships sailing along its rugged and
scenic coastline with occasional opportunities to see whales.

Access: Extremely difficult. Only via ships, such as the M. S.
Lindblad Explorer, sailing there en route to the Antarctic.

Address: None.

The South Georgia coastline in the Antarctic (photo by Donald S. Heintzelman).

Tonga

Tonga is an independent nation of more than 150 islands extending north to south over 2,000 miles (3,200 kilometers) of the southwest Pacific Ocean. The government of Tonga has established a whale sanctuary in the waters around her coastlines, and the killing of Humpback Whales in those waters now is prohibited. Additional details on watching whales in Tonga are not available.

United States of America

Alaska

Glacier Bay National Monument
Whales: Gray, Humpback, and Killer.
Viewing Season: May to September (especially June and July).
Description: A kaleidoscope of sea, glaciers, and high mountains against which whales appear in the waters of Glacier Bay. Whale watching is best done from the park headquarters area at Bartlett Cove, especially from the shoreline between the dock and Bartlett Cove campground. Additional whale watching may be done from boats and cruise ships, but such activities cause serious disturbance to whales and are now subject to special regulations. Therefore, whale watching from boats and cruise ships should not be done without first consulting with the park superintendent or his official representatives.
Access: Glacier Bay is located 100 miles (160 kilometers) northwest of Juneau. Commercial airlines, private plane charters, summer cruise ships, and private boats all are available to transport visitors to this splendid national monument.
Address: Superintendent, Glacier Bay National Monument, P. O. Box 1089, Juneau, Alaska 99802.

California

Año Nuevo State Reserve (near Santa Cruz)
Whales: Gray.
Viewing Season: December through April.
Description: Elevated vistas overlooking coastal waters in which Gray Whales migrate along the coastline.
Access: From Santa Cruz, drive north on State Highway 1 for a number of miles to the reserve which is located about halfway between Santa Cruz and Half Moon Bay.
Address: California Department of Parks and Recreation, P. O. Box 2390, Sacramento, California 95811.

Atascadero State Beach (near Morro Bay)
Whales: Gray.
Viewing Season: December and January.
Description: Headlands, cliffs, and bluffs along the coast in the vicinity of the beach where whale spouts can be seen in the coastal waters.

Access: From Atascadero, drive west on Route 41 to the junction
with State Highway 1. Turn north onto State Highway 1 and
continue to Morro Bay, then about 3 miles (4.8 kilometers) farther north on this highway to Atascadero State Beach. Observe
from there.

Address: California Department of Parks and Recreation, P. O. Box
2390, Sacramento, California 95811.

The whale observatory at Cabrillo National Monument, California (photo courtesy
of Cabrillo National Monument).

Cabrillo National Monument (San Diego)

Whales: Gray.

Viewing Season: December through February. Mid-January is the
peak whale migration viewing period.

Description: An overlook equipped with a building that serves as a
whale observatory, 300 feet south of the Old Point Loma lighthouse. During the whale migration season, park rangers are
stationed at the overlook to aid visitors in finding Gray Whales
passing just beyond the kelp beds. A short talk and a motion
picture about the Gray Whale are also provided in the auditorium during the migration months. Various free literature on
whale watching also is available.

Access: In San Diego, drive west on State Highway 209 to the end of
Point Loma. Cabrillo National Monument is located at the terminus of the road.

Address: Superintendent, Cabrillo National Monument, P. O. Box
6175, San Diego, California 92106.

Clam Beach (near Eureka)

Whales: Gray.

Viewing Season: December through April.

Description: Observations are made from Vista Point from which whale watchers can see whales and whale spouts in coastal waters.

Access: From Eureka, drive north on U. S. Route 101 for about 12 miles (19.2 kilometers) to the town of Clam Beach. Inquire locally for additional directions to Vista Point from which whale watching is done.

Address: None.

Fort Ross State Historic Park (near Jenner)

Whales: Gray.

Viewing Season: December through April.

Description: Exposed vistas providing whale watchers with views of coastal waters in which Gray Whales migrate along the coast.

Access: From Jenner, drive north on State Highway 1 for 12.6 miles (20.2 kilometers) to the park.

Address: Fort Ross State Historic Park, c/o Russian River Area, P. O. Box 123, Duncan Mills, California 95430.

Gray Whale Cove State Beach (near Pacifica)

Whales: Gray.

Viewing Season: December and January.

Description: High exposed areas from which views of the Pacific Ocean and whales in coastal waters are enjoyed.

Access: From Pacifica on State Highway 1, drive south a short distance to the entrance to Gray Whale Cove State Beach. Then continue to the parking lot.

Address: San Mateo Coast Area Headquarters, 95 Kelly Ave., Half Moon Bay, California 94019.

Gualala Head County Park (near Gualala)

Whales: Gray.

Viewing Season: December through March.

Description: High exposed areas, overlooking the sea near the mouth of the Gualala River, from which migrating Gray Whales can be seen in coastal waters.

Access: From Gualala, drive south a short distance on State Route 1 and follow signs to the park.

Address: Gualala Head County Park, P. O. Box 95, Gualala, California 95445.

Los Angeles Harbor
Whales: Gray; also Killer and Pilot.
Viewing Season: January through March.
Description: The harbor waters outside the Los Angeles breakwater, particularly the inshore waters of San Pedro Bay from the East end of Long Beach breakwater (East) to Redondo Beach Pier (West).
Access: Via Whalewatch boats leaving daily from Los Angeles Harbor, Long Beach Harbor, and Redondo Beach. All such boats and whale-watching trips are coordinated and organized through Cabrillo Marine Museum, to which interested persons should inquire. Special lectures for organized groups and schools are available via prior appointment with this museum.
Address: Cabrillo Marine Museum, 3720 Stephen White Drive, San Pedro, California 90731. Telephone (213) 548-7562.

Whale watchers in Los Angeles harbor (photo courtesy of Los Angeles Recreation and Park Department).

MacKerricher State Park (near Fort Bragg)
Whales: Gray; Killer (occasionally).
Viewing Season: December through April.
Description: Observations are made from Laguna Point in the park on flat, grass-covered headlands.
Access: From Fort Bragg in northern California, drive north on State Highway 1 for about 3 miles (4.8 kilometers) to the en-

trance to MacKerricher State Park. Enter and continue to Laguna Point.

Address: MacKerricher State Park, Mendocino Area, P. O. Box 440, Mendocino, California 95460.

Mendocino Headlands State Park (near Mendocino)

Whales: Gray; Killer (occasionally).

Viewing Season: December through April.

Description: Flat, grass-covered headlands overlooking the Pacific Ocean.

Access: From the town of Mendocino in northern California, continue a short distance on State Highway 1 to the park at the end of Little Lake Road, Mendocino Village.

Address: Mendocino Headlands State Park, Mendocino Area, P. O. Box 440, Mendocino, California 95460.

Montana de Oro State Park (near Morro Bay)

Whales: Gray.

Viewing Season: December through April.

Description: High exposed areas providing whale watchers with vantage points from which to see whale spouts and whales in coastal waters.

Access: From Morro Bay on State Highway 1, drive south a few miles, then west on a secondary road following signs to Montana de Oro State Park.

Address: Montana de Oro State Park, c/o San Luis Obispo Coast Area, 20-A Higuera Street, San Luis Obispo, California 93401.

Pigeon Point (near Pescadero)

Whales: Gray.

Viewing Season: December and January.

Description: High exposed areas from which views of the Pacific Ocean's coastal waters and whales are enjoyed.

Access: From the vicinity of Pescadero, drive south on State Highway 1 for a few miles past Bean Hollow State Beach to the parking lot at Pigeon Point.

Address: San Mateo Coast Area State Park Headquarters, 95 Kelly Avenue, Half Moon Bay, California 94019.

Point Arena Area

Whales: Gray.

Viewing Season: December to April.

Description: Exposed areas at Lighthouse Point.

Access: From the town of Point Arena on State Highway 1, seek local directions to Lighthouse Point from which whale watching is done.

Address: None.

Point Lobos State Reserve Area (near Carmel)

Whales: Gray.

Viewing Season: December and January.

Description: Bluffs, cliffs, and headlands along the coast from which whale watchers can observe whale spouts and whales in the coastal waters.

Access: From Carmel, drive south on State Highway 1 for a few miles to the entrance to Point Lobos State Reserve from whose grounds whale watching is possible. Additional whale watching is possible from bluffs, headlands, cliffs, and other roadside pull-overs along State Highway 1 as far south as Point Sur 27 miles (43.2 kilometers) south of Monterey.

Address: Point Lobos State Reserve, c/o Monterey Area, 210 Olivier Street, Monterey, California 93940.

Point Reyes National Seashore (Point Reyes)

Whales: Gray.

Viewing Season: December through February; March through May.

Description: The headlands at the Sea Lion Overlook, the Chimney Rock area, from Point Reyes Beach South, or from the observation platform at the Point Reyes lighthouse. Free whale information and park maps are available at the park headquarters.

Access: From Olema at the junction on State Highway 1 and Bear Valley Road, follow Bear Valley Road into the park to Sir Frances Drake Highway, then west on the Drake highway to the observation sites mentioned. Observe from those locations.

Address: Superintendent, Point Reyes National Seashore, Point Reyes, California 94956.

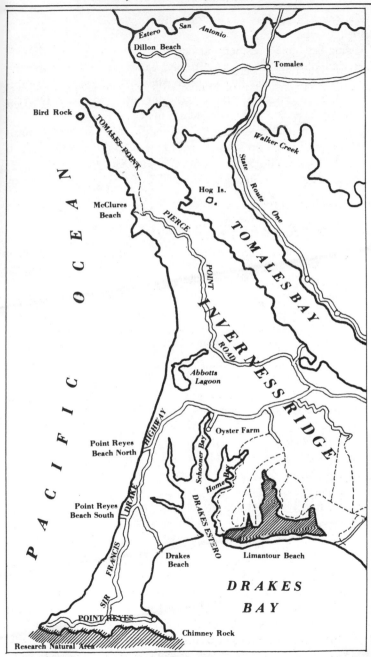

Point Reyes National Seashore, California.

Salt Point State Park (north of Jenner)

Whales: Gray.

Viewing Season: December and January.

Description: Sheer sandstone cliffs and bluffs from which observers look over the Pacific Ocean for whales. The Gerstle Cove section of the park is recommended for whale watching. Observe from atop the cliffs overlooking the cove.

Access: From Jenner, drive about 18 miles (28.8 kilometers) north on State Highway 1 to the park entrance. Then continue into the park to the parking lot overlooking Gerstle Cove.

Address: Salt Point State Park, 25050 Coast Highway 1, Jenner, California 95450.

San Simeon Coast (near San Simeon)

Whales: Gray.

Viewing Season: December and January.

Description: Bluffs, headlands, cliffs, and roadside overlooks along State Highway 1. Look for whales and whale spouts in the nearby coastal waters.

Access: From San Simeon, drive north or south along State Highway 1. Stop at various vantage points to search for whales. Binoculars are recommended.

Address: None.

Sonoma Coast State Beach (near Carmet)

Whales: Gray.

Viewing Season: December and January.

Description: Rugged headlands overlooking the Pacific Ocean. The Bodega Head section of the park is especially productive as a whale-watching lookout.

Access: From Jenner or Carmet in northern California, drive south on State Highway 1 to the Bodega Bay–Bodega Head section of the beach and continue to the parking lot at the point.

Address: Sonoma Coast State Beach, P. O. Box 385, Guerneville, California 95446.

Stillwater Cove County Park (near Fort Ross)

Whales: Gray.

Viewing Season: January through March.

Description: Exposed areas overlooking the Pacific Ocean from which migrating whales can be seen in coastal waters.

Access: From Fort Ross, drive north on State Highway 1 for about
3.5 miles (5.6 kilometers), then follow signs to the park.
Address: Stillwater Cove County Park, c/o Sonoma County Park
Department, Sonoma County Court House, Santa Rosa, California 95402.

Thornton State Beach (near Daly City)
Whales: Gray.
Viewing Season: December and January.
Description: Elevated areas providing views of the Pacific Ocean
and its coastal waters in which migrating whales appear.
Access: From San Francisco or Daly City, drive south on State Highway 1 to Alemany Boulevard and follow it to the end where
Thornton State Beach is located. A parking lot is available for
easy automobile access.
Access: San Mateo Coast Area Headquarters, 95 Kelly Avenue, Half
Moon Bay, California 94019.

Hawaii

Watching whales is an extremely productive and popular activity in some of the Hawaiian Islands. It is possible to do so from various land lookouts as well as from many hotels and condominiums on
the western side of Maui, including those at Kihei and Wailea, and
thus avoid disturbing the mammals in the water. Humpback Whales
are the marine mammals most commonly seen. In addition to the
whale-watching lookouts and other areas, officials of Maui County
also have established a unique reserve for whales in the waters
around Maui: the Maui County Whale Reserve. Persons wishing
more information about this reserve and whale watching and conservation in general in the Hawaiian Islands are urged to contact the
Lahaina Restoration Foundation, P. O. Box 338, Lahaina, Maui,
Hawaii 96761. While in the islands, a visit to that fine institution's
museum, the Brig Carthaginian, is another worthwhile activity.

Honolua Bay (on Maui Highway #30 near Honokohau)
Whales: Humpback; Sperm and Pilot occasionally.
Viewing Season: November to June, with the best whale-watching
opportunities in late February.
Description: A drive-in roadside lookout providing views of whales

in the Pailolo Channel (part of the Maui County Whale Reserve).

Access: From Lahaina, follow Highway #30, the main coast road, 10 miles (16 kilometers) to the drive-in lookout above Honolua Bay. Observe from there with binoculars.

Address: Lahaina Restoration Foundation, P. O. Box 338, Lahaina, Maui, Hawaii 96761.

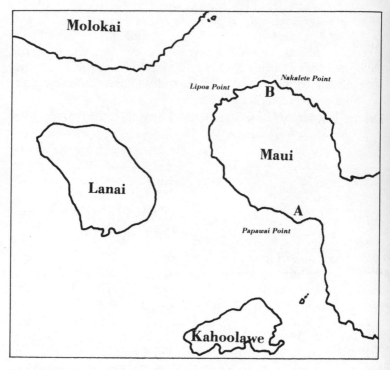

The Maui County Whale Reserve, Hawaii.

Kauai's Southern Coast

Whales: Humpback; Sperm and Pilot occasionally.

Viewing Season: November to June, with the best whale-watching opportunities in late February.

Description: Any high, exposed headland, cliff, or bluff from which one can survey the waters surrounding the island. Humpback Whales occur in these waters and can be seen from time to time with the aid of binoculars.

Access: Follow any road along the coastline of the southern portion of Kauai and stop to look for whales at spots from which views of the surrounding waters can be seen.

Address: None.

Kona Coast (on Big Island of Hawaii)

Whales: Humpback; Sperm and Pilot occasionally.

Viewing Season: November to June, with the best whale-watching opportunities in late February.

Description: The coastal waters off the Kona coast along the western side of the Big Island of Hawaii. Any high, exposed headland, cliff, or bluff can be used if the surrounding waters can be observed with binoculars. Humpback Whales occur in these waters and can be seen from time to time with the aid of binoculars.

Access: Follow any coast road along the western side of the Big Island of Hawaii along the Kona Coast, which is located on the southern half of the island.

Address: None.

Oahu's Leeward Coast

Whales: Humpback; Sperm and Pilot occasionally.

Viewing Season: November to June, with the best whale-watching opportunities in late February.

Description: Any high, exposed headland, cliff, or bluff from which one can look over the waters surrounding the leeward side of the island. Humpback Whales occur in these waters and can be seen from time to time with the aid of binoculars.

Access: Follow any coastal roads along the leeward side of the island. Stop at suitable points from which the coastal waters along the coastline can be seen and scanned with the aid of binoculars.

Address: None.

Pali Lookout (on Maui Highway #30 near Maalaea)

Whales: Humpback; Sperm and Pilot occasionally.

Viewing Season: November to June, with the best whale-watching opportunities in late February.

Description: A drive-in roadside lookout providing views of whales in a recognized calving ground in Maalaea Bay (part of the Maui County Whale Reserve) and waters between the western side of Maui and the island of Lanai. A memorial plaque dedicated to the Humpback Whale marks this lookout.

Access: From Lahaina, drive southeast along the coast road (Highway #30) along the western side of Maui to the Pali Lookout, beside the road, near Maalaea. Drive carefully in this area during the peak of the whale-watching season because of frequent whale traffic jams. Use binoculars.

Address: Lahaina Restoration Foundation, P. O. Box 338, Lahaina, Maui, Hawaii 96761.

Maine

Observations of whales, dolphins, and porpoises in the Gulf of Maine (Cape Cod to Nova Scotia) are collected, coordinated, and studied by the Gulf of Maine Whale Sighting Network (College of the Atlantic, Bar Harbor, Maine 04609). Persons who see or photograph whales and other cetaceans in the Gulf of Maine are asked to send details of their observations or copies of photographs taken to the network office at the address provided above. Photographs of the flukes of Humpback Whales are especially desired.

Gulf of Maine Ferry Boats

Whales: Fin, Humpback, Minke, Black Right, Killer, and Pilot. On rare occasions other species also appear.

Viewing Season: April through November.

Description: The open waters of the Gulf of Maine.

Access: Via the ferry M/V *Bluenose* running between Bar Harbor, Maine and Yarmouth, Nova Scotia, or the M/V *Bolero* or M/V *Prince of Fundy* running between Portland, Maine and Yarmouth, Nova Scotia.

Address: None.

Monhegan Island (off Port Clyde)
Whales: Fin, Humpback, sometimes other species.
Viewing Season: April through November.
Description: A charming, offshore island from which whale watching is possible from the island's central high point or from the various cliffs, bluffs, and headlands around the shoreline.
Access: Via ferry from Port Clyde, Maine. Overnight accomodations are available on the island. Contact your local travel agent for details about lodging and meals.
Address: None.

Mount Desert Rock
Whales: Minke, Fin, Humpback, Black Right, Killer, and Pilot.
Viewing Season: April through November.
Description: A small, rocky island located about 20 miles (32 kilometers) south of Mount Desert Island, Maine, in the Gulf of Maine. Whale watchers associated with Allied Whale maintain an annual research whale watch in cooperation with a Coast Guard facility on the island. However, landing on the island is prohibited. Whales are readily observed from the island's offshore waters, but mooring boats to the Coast Guard's buoy also is prohibited.
Access: Only via boat after special arrangements are made with the scientists from Allied Whale. Generally such visits are made for research purposes only.
Address: Allied Whale, College of the Atlantic, Bar Harbor, Maine 04609.

A Humpback Whale diving off Mt. Desert Rock, Maine (photo by Steven Katona).

Pemaquid Point (near Damariscotta)

Whales: Fin; rarely Killer.

Viewing Season: July, particularly late July.

Description: A beautiful, surf-lashed rocky point from which views of whales sometimes are enjoyed offshore.

Access: From the junction of U. S. Route 1 and State Route 129 and 130 at Damariscotta, drive south on State Route 130 to its terminus at the parking lot at Pemaquid Point. Park there, then walk a short distance to the rugged, rocky point from which whale watching is possible with the aid of binoculars.

Address: None.

Quoddy Head State Park (near Lubec)

Whales: Fin, Humpback, and Sperm.

Viewing Season: July through September.

Description: A rocky shoreline with much surf and views of coastal waters. Whale watching at this site is not always exceptionally productive but sometimes can be exciting.

Access: From West Lubec, drive east on State Route 189 for a few miles to a road west of Lubec, then turn south onto this un-numbered road and continue for a few miles to the park entrance. Signs point to the park along parts of the road. The location of the park also is shown on most Maine road maps.

Address: Manager, Quoddy Head State Park, Lubec, Maine 04632.

Maryland

Baltimore and Washington Canyons (off Ocean City)

Whales: Fin, Minke (very rarely), Sperm, and Pilot. Also Atlantic Spotted Dolphin, Common Dolphin, Risso's Dolphin, Bottle-nosed Dolphin, and White-Sided Dolphin.

Viewing Season: April to June; August. April is particularly good for marine mammal viewing.

Description: Open western north Atlantic Ocean waters from 5 to 60 miles offshore to the edge of the Baltimore and Washington Canyons. Observations are made from the decks of the fishing boat *Mariner* which departs (by advance reservations only) from the Talbot Street Pier, Talbot Street at the Bay, Ocean City, Maryland.

Access: Via deep-sea fishing boats departing from Ocean City, Maryland. All arrangements are made through Richard A. Rowlett.

Address: Richard A. Rowlett, P. O. Box 579, Ocean City, Maryland
21842.

Massachusetts

Race Point (near Provincetown)
Whales: Fin, Humpback, Black Right; Harbor Porpoise.
Viewing Season: April through July; September through November.
Description: A moderately low dune area overlooking Cape Cod Bay
from which whales sometimes are seen not far from shore.
Access: In Provincetown at the outer tip of Cape Cod, follow
U. S. Route 6 to Race Point Road. Turn left onto Race Point
Road and continue to the visitors' center where additional de-
tails about whale watching at Race Point can be secured.
Address: None.

Stellwagen Bank (off Cape Cod)
Whales: Minke, Fin, Humpback, Black Right, Killer, Pilot; also
Atlantic White-Sided Dolphin, White-beaked Dolphin, Har-
bor Porpoise.
Viewing Season: April to October.
Description: Open waters over Stellwagen Bank, northwest of the tip
of Cape Cod. Whale watching is done from the decks of boats
such as the *Dolphin III* and the *Ranger III,* both of which are
well known for their whale-watching activities.
Access: Via boat from Provincetown near the tip of Cape Cod.
Address: Captain Al Avellar, *Dolphin III,* Box 162, Eastham,
Massachusetts 02642; Jerry Costa, *Ranger III,* 29 Standish St.,
Provincetown, Massachusetts 02657.

New Hampshire

Jeffreys' Ledge
Whales: Fin, Humpback, and Black Right.
Viewing Season: Spring and autumn.
Description: A ledge about 20 miles in the Atlantic Ocean off Ports-
mouth, New Hampshire. Whale watching is done from the
decks of the M/V *Viking Queen* and is coordinated and super-
vised by Allied Whale.
Access: Via boat from Portsmouth, New Hampshire, with arrange-
ments made through Allied Whale, College of the Atlantic,
Bar Harbor, Maine.
Address: Allied Whale, College of the Atlantic, Bar Harbor,
Maine 04609.

New Jersey

Hudson Canyon (off Brigantine)

Whales: Fin, Minke (very rarely), Sei, Black Right, Sperm, and Pilot; also Common Dolphin and Risso's Dolphin.

Viewing Season: April to June; perhaps year-round.

Description: Open western north Atlantic Ocean about 90 miles off the New Jersey coast over the Hudson Canyon. Observations are made from the decks of fishing boats such as those used for pelagic bird-watching purposes.

Access: Via fishing boats departing from Atlantic Highlands and Brielle, New Jersey.

Address: Delaware Valley Ornithological Club, c/o Academy of Natural Sciences of Philadelphia, 19th and The Parkway, Philadelphia, Pennsylvania 19103; Marine Mammal Stranding Center, Historic Gardner's Basin, North New Hampshire Avenue, Atlantic City, New Jersey 08401.

Oregon

Brookings Area

Whales: Gray, Killer (rarely).

Viewing Season: March and April.

Description: Bluffs in the vicinity of the jetty and other high vantage points from which whales can be seen in coastal waters.

Access: From Brookings, drive along U. S. Route 101 and stop for whale-watching purposes at various roadside pull-overs along the highway.

Address: Leo's Sporthaven Marina, Box 2215, Brookings, Oregon 97415.

Cape Blanco (near Langlois and Port Orford)

Whales: Gray, Killer (rare).

Viewing Season: December through April.

Description: Exposed areas near the lighthouse provide whale watchers with suitable observation sites from which to see whales in coastal waters.

Access: From Langlois, drive south on U. S. Route 101 for a few miles to the road leading to the Cape Blanco lighthouse. Turn onto that road and continue to the lighthouse from which observations are made. Alternatively, from Port Orford, drive north on U. S. Route 101 for a few miles to the road leading to the lighthouse and continue on that access road to the Cape

Blanco lighthouse from which whale watching also is done.
Address: None.

Fort Stevens State Park (near Astoria)
Whales: Gray, Killer.
Viewing Season: December through May.
Description: Bluffs, headlands, cliffs, and other elevated spots from
    which it is possible to see whales in coastal waters.
Access: From Astoria on U. S. Routes 26/101, follow signs north-
    ward on secondary roads to the entrance to Fort Stevens State
    Park from which whale watching is possible.
Address: Superintendent, Fort Stevens State Park, Box 173, Ham-
    mond, Oregon 97121.

Port Orford
Whales: Gray, Killer.
Viewing Season: March and April (for Gray Whales); Killer Whales
    are observed from time to time at other seasons of the year.
Description: Any exposed area such as cliffs, bluffs, headlands, and
    other elevated sites from which it is possible to look for whales
    in coastal waters.
Access: Port Orford is reached readily by driving along U. S. Route
    101 which runs along the Oregon coastline.
Address: None.

Yachats Area (near Newport)
Whales: Gray.
Viewing Season: December through April.
Description: Elevated coastal sites on Cape Perpetua and Strawberry
    Hill located about 3 miles (4.8 kilometers) from Yachats.
Access: From Newport on U. S. Route 101, drive south on that high-
    way for a few miles to the Yachats area from which whale
    watching is enjoyed.
Address: None.

Washington

Dungeness State Park Area (near Port Angeles)
Whales: Killer.
Viewing Season: All seasons but never consistently.
Description: Killer Whales are sometimes seen just beyond the kelp
    beds in the Strait of Juan de Fuca from the vicinity of Dunge-

ness State Park (east of Port Angeles) westward to Neah Bay at
the northwestern tip of the Olympic peninsula and the terminus of State Route 112. Viewing can be done from any elevated site, providing a good view of the Strait of Juan de Fuca
to the north.

Access: From Port Angeles, drive westward on U. S. Route 101 to
the junction with State Route 112, then continue westward on
that road (Route 112) to Neah Bay. Stop at suitable roadside
observation sites to look for whales just beyond the kelp beds
along the shoreline.

Address: None.

Cape Flattery Area (near Neah Bay)

Whales: Gray, Killer (occasionally).

Viewing Season: March through May.

Description: Cliffs, bluffs, headlands, and other elevated sites from
which whale watchers can look westward over the coastal
waters for marine mammals.

Access: From Port Angeles, drive west on U. S. Route 101 to the
junction with State Route 112, then continue west on State
Route 112 to the town of Neah Bay. From there, secure local
directions for visiting the outer (northwestern) end of Cape
Flattery.

Address: None.

Ocean Shores Area (near Aberdeen)

Whales: Gray, Humpback, Killer.

Viewing Season: March through May and October through
November.

Description: Any elevated site along the coastline from which
whales and whale spouts can be seen in the coastal waters.

Access: From Aberdeen, drive west on U. S. Route 12 to the junction with U. S. Route 101. Follow U. S. Route 101 for a few
miles to the junction with State Route 109. There continue
westward on State Route 109 to Ocean City. At that community drive southward on another road, following local road
signs, to the tip of the peninsula extending into Gray's Harbor.
Stop from time to time at suitable roadside pull-overs for
whale watching.

Address: None.

Olympic National Park (near Queets)

Whales: Minke, Humpback, Gray, Sperm, Killer, Pilot; also Dall's Porpoise.

Viewing Season: March through May and October through November.

Description: Numerous headlands, cliffs, bluffs, and other elevated sites along U. S. Route 101 as it passes along the coastline. Whales can be seen from most of these spots if one selects a location with a good view of coastal waters and spends a day of careful observation. The Kalaloch area near the Kalaloch Ranger Station is well suited for whale watching and is easily visited.

Access: From Queets, drive north on U. S. Route 101 for a number of miles. En route stop at various sites along the highway, including the Kalaloch area, from which one looks over coastal waters in which whales and whale spouts can be seen. Gray Whales are the most likely species to be seen.

Address: Superintendent, Olympic National Park, 600 East Park Avenue, Port Angeles, Washington 98362.

6
GLOSSARY

baleen plates Long, horny or fiber-like structures, each from 2 to 14 feet long, growing in separate plates from the gums of the upper jaws of the so-called baleen whales. The structures or plates form a mat and serve as a large filter which traps krill inside the whale's mouth as water is expelled through the baleen plates.

beak The elongated forward or anterior portion of the head of certain cetaceans such as the so-called beaked whales.

blowhole The nostrils or openings on the back of whales and other cetaceans through which the animals breathe. They expel air through the blowholes, via spouting or blowing, when they surface.

bonnet Horn-like, crusty growths on the top of the upper jaw and part of the head of Black Right Whales.

breaching A behavior pattern of whales whereby the animals burst out of the water, briefly expose their bodies to view, then fall back into the water again.

bubble net An underwater net constructed by a Humpback Whale of a large number of bubbles placed in a ring. The net traps krill which is then eaten by the whale. Humpback Whales apparently are fully capable of selecting the size of the bubbles they produce to make the nets; thus, they determine at will the size of the net's mesh.

care-giving behavior A behavior pattern similar to human kindness or altruism occasionally displayed by some species of whales such as Killer Whales. An example is the effort of a pair of Killer Whales that cradled an injured calf between them to prevent it from turning upside down in the water.

coastal waters Waters extending from a coastline outward to a distance of about 50 miles (80 kilometers) offshore.

dorsal fin The elevated fin-like structure on the back of some cetaceans.

dorsal ridge A somewhat elevated area on the back of some cetaceans either replacing a dorsal fin or serving as a base for a small dorsal fin.

flick feeding A feeding technique used by Humpback Whales whereby they use their flukes to splash water over their heads. As the water lands in front of the whales, the cetaceans swim into the splash and gulp the water, in which is contained krill.

flipper The anterior or forward appendages of cetaceans which replace the arms and hands in man.

flukes The posterior or rear appendages of cetaceans.

herd A group of whales or other cetaceans.

jet *See* **spout.**

jump *See* **breach.**

krill Small species of invertebrate marine life, found in enormous numbers, which forms major food items for some species of whales such as the baleen whales.

marine waters Waters extending from 150 to 200 miles (240 to 320 kilometers) offshore.

melon The bulbous forehead on some whales, dolphins, and porpoises. It apparently is closely associated with sonar or echolocation in cetaceans, especially in those species in which the melon is particularly large and well developed.

pelagic waters Deep oceanic waters more than 200 miles (320 kilometers) offshore.

pod A group or herd of whales numbering two or more animals.

saddle The gray mark on the back of Killer Whales immediately behind the dorsal fin.

snout The forward portion of the lower jaw in beaked whales and certain other cetaceans.

sparing Behavior used by some species of whales, including Gray Whales, in which they push their heads above the surface of the water and look around for brief periods of time.

spout Air expelled through the blowhole(s) of whales or other cetaceans when they surface to breathe.

spy-outing *See* **sparing.**

strandings Cetaceans, generally whales, that beach themselves or otherwise come ashore along beaches or other coastlines. The reasons for such strandings are poorly understood.

whalebone *See* **baleen plates.**

7

APPENDIX

Whale Conservation Organizations

In addition to the many well-known national conservation organizations, all of which support the protection and conservation of whales and other cetaceans, the following organizations are especially concerned with whale conservation and/or research and deserve widespread public support.

Allied Whale
College of the Atlantic
Bar Harbor, Maine 04609

American Cetacean Society
P. O. Box 4416
San Pedro, California 90731

Cabrillo Marine Museum
3720 Stephen White Drive
San Pedro, California 90731

Cetacean Defense League
Box 14109
Santa Barbara, California 93106

Cetacean Research Associates
1592 Sunset Cliffs Drive
San Diego, California 92107

Connecticut Cetacean Society
190 Stillwold
Wethersfield, Connecticut 06109

Cousteau Society
777 Third Avenue
New York, New York 10017

Fin Alliance
36 Lexington Avenue
Suffern, New York 10901

General Whale
P. O. Box "Save the Whale"
Alameda, California 94501

Greenpeace Foundation
240 Fort Mason
San Francisco, California 94107

Humpback Whale Survey
Box 139
Holualoa, Hawaii 96725

Lahaina Restoration Foundation
P. O. Box 338
Lahaina, Maui, Hawaii 96761

Marine Mammal Stranding Center
Historic Gardner's Basin
North New Hampshire Avenue
Atlantic City, New Jersey 08401

Maui Whalewatchers
Box 457
Lahaina, Maui, Hawaii 96761

Mendocino Whale War
P. O. Box 383
Mendocino, California 95460

Mingan Island Cetacean Study
50 Portside Circle
East Falmouth, Massachusetts 02536

Ocean Research and Education Society
51 Commercial Wharf
Denton, Massachusetts 02110

Oceanic Society
Stamford Marine Center
Magee Avenue
Stamford, Connecticut 06902

Orca Survey Research Station
Route 1, Box 181X
Friday Harbor, Washington 98250

Project Jonah
P. O. Box 40280
San Francisco, California 94140

Rare Animal Relief Effort Inc.
c/o National Audubon Society
950 Third Avenue
New York, New York 10022

Save the Dolphins
1945 20th Avenue
San Francisco, California 94116

Save Our Whales
6351 North Oakley
Chicago, Illinois 60659

Save the Whales Hawaii
404 Piikoi Street, Room 209
Honolulu, Hawaii 06814

The Whale Center
3929 Piedmont Avenue
Oakland, California 94611

Whale Fund
New York Zoological Society
New York Zoological Park
Bronx, New York 10460

Whale Protection Fund
1925 K Street, N. W.
Washington, D. C. 20006

The Whale Museum
Box 1154
Friday Harbor, Washington 98250

Whales Unlimited
21 Laurel Hill Road
Ridgefield, Connecticut 06877

World Wildlife Fund
1319 18th Street, N. W.
Washington, D. C. 20036

Member Nations of the International Whaling Commission

As the major international body responsible for the conservation, management, and use of whales, the International Whaling Commission (The Red House, Station Road, Histon, Cambridge, England CB4 4NP) is embodied with the power to stop the slaughter of all whales around the globe. To date, it has not done so. Persons wishing to protest the actions of the IWC can do so directly at their address. Alternatively, they can contact officials of the following member nations of the IWC and inform them of their views and concerns regarding whales and their protection:

Argentina	New Zealand
Australia	Norway
Brazil	Panama
Canada	Peru
Chile	Seychelles
Denmark	South Africa
France	Spain
Iceland	Sweden
Japan	United Kingdom
Republic of Korea	United States of America
Mexico	USSR
Netherlands	

Of the above 23 IWC member nations, the following still carry on commercial whaling despite worldwide protests against such activities:

Brazil	Republic of Korea
Chile	Norway
Denmark	Peru
Iceland	Spain
Japan	USSR

The following three non-IWC nations also engage in commercial whaling:

> China
> Cyprus
> Portugal

United States Federal Laws
and Marine Mammal Protection

Under provisions of the Endangered Species Act of 1973 and the Marine Mammal Protection Act of 1972, these activities are violations of the law.

Boats, swimmers, and divers

1. All boats, swimmers, and divers are prohibited from approaching whale calving and breeding grounds under United States control closer than 2 miles. In the Hawaiian Islands, prohibited entry areas include those within 2 miles of mean high-tide water line from Kaena Point east by southwest to Kamaiki Point on Lanai, and all waters inshore from Hekili Point at Olowalu southeast to Puu Olai, Maui.

2. An approach within 300 yards of a Humpback Whale.

3. Driving or herding a Humpback Whale from any distance.

4. In other portions (except as above) within 200 nautical miles of the Hawaiian islands, no approach can be made within 100 yards of a Humpback Whale; multiple changes in speed of vessels or moving faster than a whale (or the slowest whale in a group) while between 100 and 300 yards of the mammals; separating a whale from a calf; or driving or herding whales.

Aircraft

1. Pilots of aircraft shall not fly lower than 1,000 feet while within a horizontal distance of 300 yards from a whale.

2. Aircraft shall not hover over, circle around, or buzz whales.

General restrictions

All other acts or omissions that substantially disrupt the normal behavior of a whale is presumed to constitute whale harassment. Examples of such substantial disruption of whale behavior include:

1. The whale makes a rapid change in speed or direction.

2. The whale uses escape tactics including, but not limited to, prolonged diving, underwater course change, exhalation under water, or evasive swimming patterns.

3. The whale interrupts breeding or nursing activities.

4. The whale attempts to shield a calf from a vessel or human observer by swishing its tail or other movements.

5. The whale no longer uses an area previously frequented.

Since all restrictions are subject to change, persons may wish to contact the National Marine Fisheries Services, P. O. Box 3830, Honolulu, Hawaii 96812 for the most up-to-date details. On Oahu telephone (808) 946-2181; on Maui telephone (808) 244-7572.

For additional details on marine mammal protection contact any of the following offices:

National Marine Fisheries Service
Northeast Region
14 Elm Street
Gloucester, Massachusetts 01930

National Marine Fisheries Service
Southeast Region
9450 Gandy Blvd.
St. Petersburg, Florida 33702

National Marine Fisheries Service
Northwest Region
1700 Westlake Avenue, North
Seattle, Washington 98109

National Marine Fisheries Service
Southwest Region
300 South Ferry St.
Terminal Island, California 90731

National Marine Fisheries Service
Alaska Region
709 West 9th St.
Juneau, Alaska 99801

Recent Estimates of
Numbers of Great Whales

Species	Estimated numbers surviving 1976	1979
Minke Whale	300,000	300,000
Sei Whale	75,000	75,000
Bryde's Whale	40,000	Unknown
Blue Whale	13,000	10,000 to 13,000
Fin Whale	100,000	100,000
Humpback Whale	7,000	7,000
Bowhead Whale	2,000?	1,800 to 2,800
Black Right Whale	4,000?	1,000 to 4,000
Gray Whale	11,000	14,000 to 18,000
Sperm Whale (males)	230,000	230,000
Sperm Whale (females)	390,000	390,000

Source. 1976 data from V. B. Scheffer in *National Geographic*, 1976; 755; 1979 data in M. Payne in *The Living Wilderness*, 1979, 43 (147): 17.

Whale Sighting Report Forms

WHALEWATCH OBSERVATIONAL DATA

(Use one sheet for each sighting)

AMERICAN CETACEAN SOCIETY   CABRILLO MARINE MUSEUM VOLUNTEERS
****

Date _____ Day of Week _____

Vessel_____ Skipper_____ Observer _____

Home Port _____

Departure time _____ Time returned _____

Names of other whalewatch boats observing this sighting _____

_____

1. Number of whales sighted _____

2. Time of sighting _____ to _____

3. Log the following information on the chart (over)

    a. Location (direction & distance from landmark)

4. South _____ or North _____ bound.

5. Fathometer reading _____

6. Number of mother-calf pairs _____

7. Number of calves _____

8. Special behaviors & observations (circle letter and discuss if pos-
    sible.

    a. Spyhooping   e. Nursing   h. Tags or unusual
    b. Feeding   f. Swim patterns   marks
    c. Breaching   g. Surfacing with   i. No flukes show on
    d. Mating   no-blow   deep dive
                                               j. Other

9. Gray whale associations with other animals (birds, dolphins, sea
    lions, etc...)

Prepared By Wm F. Samaras

Courtesy Cabrillo Marine Museum.

Whale Sighting Report Forms

SIGHTING REPORT

DATE AND LOCAL TIME

_____

LOCATION (LATITUDE AND LONGITUDE)

_____

IDENTIFICATION

     Common name _____

     Scientific name _____

NUMBER OF ANIMALS SIGHTED

_____

HEADING OF ANIMAL(S) (MAGNETIC)

_____

ESTIMATED SPEED (KNOTS)

_____

ASSOCIATED BIRDS OR FISHES

_____

_____

TAGS

_____

_____

REMARKS

_____

_____

_____

_____

Courtesy National Marine Fisheries Service.

Whale Sighting Report Forms

MARINE MAMMAL SIGHTING FORM
* DO NOT FILL IN BOXES PRECEDED BY AN ASTERISK

1. NAME _____   RECORD ID * ☐☐☐☐☐☐
   VESSEL _____   1 2 3 4 5 6

2. DATE (Yr./Mo./Day) & TIME (local) OF SIGHTING ☐☐☐☐☐☐   ☐☐☐☐
                                                  7 8 9 10 11 12   13 14 15 16

3. LATITUDE (degrees/minutes/10ths)—N/S   ☐☐☐☐☐   ☐
                                            18 19 20 21 22   23

4. LONGITUDE (degrees/minutes/10ths)—E/W   ☐☐☐☐☐☐   ☐
                                             24 25 26 27 28 29   30

5. SPECIES _____ _____ * ☐☐ TENTATIVE * ☐
           Common name   Scientific name   33 34   35

6. NUMBER SIGHTED _____ ± _____   C.I. * ☐   ☐☐☐☐
                                                    36   37 38 39 40

7. GROUP SIZE ☐☐   8. DIRECTION HEADED ☐☐ * ☐☐
              41 42   43 44   45 46

9. ANGLE FROM BOW ☐☐   10. INITIAL SIGHTING DISTANCE _____
   (10's of degrees) 47 48

                                              10's of meters ☐☐☐
                                                             49 50 51

11. VISIBILITY _____   12. SEA STATE (Beaufort) _____ VIS CODE * ☐
                                                                             52

13. WEATHER _____   14. SEA SURFACE TEMP (° C) ± ☐ ☐☐
                                                          53   54 55

   PLATFORM CODE * ☐☐☐☐   15. TIME ZONE ± ☐ ☐☐
                  56 57 58 59   60   61 62

16. How did you identify animal(s)? Sketch and describe animal; associated organisms;
    behavior (include closest approach); comments.

GPO 989-609   * ☐☐☐☐☐☐☐☐☐☐☐☐☐☐☐☐☐
                 64 65 66 67 68 69 70 71 72 73 74 75 76 77 78 79 80

Courtesy National Marine Mammal Laboratory.

Whale Sighting Report Forms

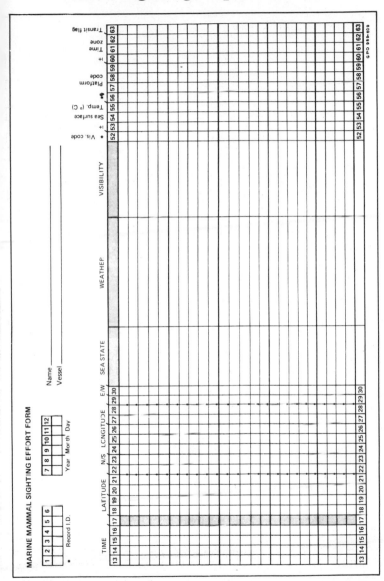

Courtesy National Marine Mammal Laboratory.

Whale Sighting Report Forms

ADDITIONAL INFORMATION -

VESSEL NAME & NUMBER _____

PRINCIPAL OBSERVER(S) _____

ADDRESS   _____

             _____

             _____

CRUISE SPEED OF VESSEL _____   MAX. SPEED _____

HEIGHT OF EYE ABOVE SEA SURFACE FOR EACH OBSERVER LOCATION:

1. Bridge _____m   2. Flying Bridge _____m   3. Bow _____m

Brief description of cruise plan, vessel type, and any general comments:

Return forms and this page at the end of each cruise to:

Platforms of Opportunity Program
National Marine Mammal Laboratory, NWAFC
7600 Sand Point Way N.E. - Bldg. 32
Seattle, Washington   98115

Courtesy National Marine Mammal Laboratory.

Whale Sighting Report Forms

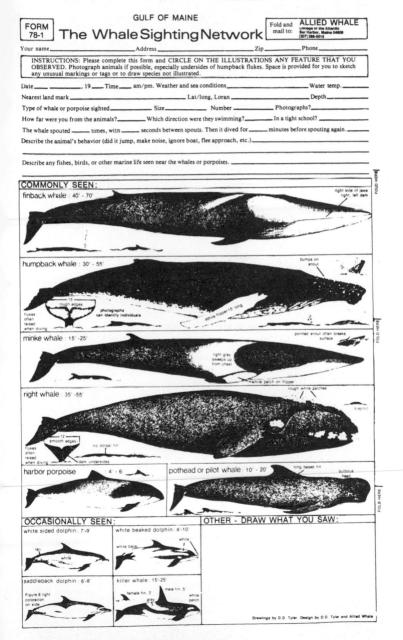

GULF OF MAINE

FORM 78-1

The Whale Sighting Network

Fold and mail to: **ALLIED WHALE** College of the Atlantic, Bar Harbor, Maine 04609 (207) 288-5015

Your name_____ Address_____ Zip_____ Phone_____

INSTRUCTIONS: Please complete this form and CIRCLE ON THE ILLUSTRATIONS ANY FEATURE THAT YOU OBSERVED. Photograph animals if possible, especially undersides of humpback flukes. Space is provided for you to sketch any unusual markings or tags or to draw species not illustrated.

Date_____ _____, 19___ Time____ am/pm. Weather and sea conditions_____ Water temp._____

Nearest land mark_____ Lat/long, Loran_____ Depth_____

Type of whale or porpoise sighted_____ Size_____ Number_____ Photographs?_____

How far were you from the animals?_____ Which direction were they swimming?_____ In a tight school?_____

The whale spouted _____ times, with _____ seconds between spouts. Then it dived for _____ minutes before spouting again._____

Describe the animal's behavior (did it jump, make noise, ignore boat, flee approach, etc.)_____

Describe any fishes, birds, or other marine life seen near the whales or porpoises._____

COMMONLY SEEN:

finback whale : 40' - 70'
right side of jaws light, left dark

humpback whale : 30' - 55'
bumps on snout
flukes often raised when diving — rough edges
photographs can identify individuals
White flipper 15' long

minke whale : 15' -25'
pointed snout often breaks surface
light gray sweeps up from chest
white patch on flipper

right whale : 35' -55'
rough white patches
V-spout
flukes often raised when diving — smooth edges
no dorsal fin
dark undersides

harbor porpoise : 4' - 6'

pothead or pilot whale : 10' - 20'
long based fin
bulbous head

OCCASIONALLY SEEN:

white sided dolphin : 7'-9'
white

white beaked dolphin : 8'-10'
white back
white

saddleback dolphin : 6'-8'
Figure 8 light coloration on side

killer whale : 15'-25'
female fin. 3'
male fin. 5'
gray
white patch

OTHER - DRAW WHAT YOU SAW:

Drawings by D.D. Tyler. Design by D.D. Tyler and Allied Whale

8
SUGGESTED READING

Alaska Geographic Society, "Alaska Whales and Whaling." *Alaska Geographic,* 5 (4): 1-114, 1978.

Alpers, A., **Dolphins: The Myth and the Mammal.** Houghton Mifflin Co., Boston, Mass., 1961.

Anderson, H. T., ed., **The Biology of Marine Mammals.** Academic Press, New York, 1969.

Burton R., **The Life and Death of Whales.** Universe Books, New York, 1973.

Caldwell, D. K., and M. C. Caldwell, **The World of the Bottlenosed Dolphin.** J. B. Lippincott Co., Philadelphia, Penn., 1972.

Coffey, D. J., **Dolphins, Whales and Porpoises: An Encyclopedia of Sea Mammals.** Macmillan Publishing Co., Inc., New York, 1977.

Cousteau, J. Y., **The Whale: Mighty Monarch of the Sea.** Doubleday & Co., Inc., New York, 1972.

Daugherty, A. E., **Marine Mammals of California.** California Department of Fish and Game, Sacramento, Calif., 1972.

Hershkovitz, P., *Catalog of Living Whales.* Bulletin 246. U. S. National Museum, Washington, D. C., 1966.

Katona, S. K., D. T. Richardson, and R. Hazard, **A Field Guide to the Whales and Seals of the Gulf of Maine.** 2nd Edition. College of the Atlantic, Bar Harbor, Maine, 1977.

Kellogg, W. N., **Porpoises and Sonar.** University of Chicago Press, Chicago, Ill., 1961.

Kraus, S., and S. Katona, **Humpback Whales** *(Megaphera novaeanglinae)* **in the North Atlantic–A Catalog of Identified Individuals.** College of the Atlantic, Bar Harbor, Maine, 1977.

Leatherwood, S., D. D. Caldwell, and H. E. Winn, *Whales, Dolphins, and Porpoises of the Wesern North Atlantic–A Guide to their Indentification.* NOAA Technical Report NMFS Circ-396. National Oceanic and Atmospheric Administration (National Marine Fisheries Service), Seattle, Washington, 1976.

Leatherwood, S., W. E. Evans, and D. W. Rice, *The Whales, Dolphins, and Porpoises of the Eastern North Pacific–A Guide to their Indentification in the Water.* Report NUC TP 282. Naval Undersea Center, San Diego, Calif., 1972.

Lockley, R. M., **Whales, Dolphins, and Porpoises.** W. W. Norton & Co., Inc., New York, 1979.

Matthews, L. H., **The Whale.** Simon and Schuster, New York, 1968.

————. **The Natural History of the Whale.** Columbia University Press, New York, 1978.

————. **Penguins, Whalers, and Sealers.** Universe Books, New York, 1978.

McIntyre, J., ed., **Mind in the Waters.** Charles Scribner's Sons, New York, 1974.

McNulty, F., **The Great Whales.** Doubleday & Co., Inc., Garden City, N. Y., 1973.

Miller, T., **The World of the California Gray Whale.** Baja Trail Publications, Inc., Santa Ana, Calif., 1975.

Mörzer Bruyns, W. F. J., **Field Guide of Whales and Dolphins.** Uitgeverij Tor, Amsterdam, Netherlands, 1971.

Murphy, R. C., **Logbook for Grace.** Macmillan Co., New York, 1947.

————. **A Dead Whale or a Stove Boat.** Houghton Mifflin Co., Boston, Mass., 1967.

National Audubon Society: Special issue devoted to whales and other cetaceans. *Audubon,* 77 (1): 1-128. January 1975.

National Geographic Society: Special issue devoted to whales. *National Geographic,* 150 (6): 722-767. December 1976. Special issue devoted to dolphins and whales. *National Geographic,* 144 (4): 506-545. April 1979.

Norman, J. R., and F. C. Fraser, **Field Book of Giant Fishes.** G. P. Putnam Co., New York, 1949.

Norris, K. S., **Whales, Dolphins, and Porpoises.** University of California Press, Berkeley, Calif., 1966.

_____. **The Porpoise Watcher.** W. W. Norton Co., New York, 1974.

Orr, R. T., *Marine Mammals of California.* California Natural History Guides No. 29. University of California Press, Berkeley, Calif., 1972.

Rice, D. W., and A. A. Wolman, *The Life History and Ecology of the Gray Whale (Eschrichtius robustus).* Special Publication No. 3. American Society of Mammalogists, 1971.

Scammon, C. M., **The Marine Mammals of the Northwestern Coast of North America.** Dover Publications, New York, 1968.

Scheffer, V. B., **The Year of the Whale.** Charles Scribner's Sons, New York, 1969.

_____. **A Natural History of Marine Mammals.** Charles Scribner's Sons, New York, 1976.

Schevill, W. E., ed., **The Whale Problem: A Status Report.** Harvard University Press, Cambridge, Mass., 1974.

Slijper, E. J., **Whales.** University of Michigan Press, Ann Arbor, Mich., 1976.

Small, G. L., **The Blue Whale.** Columbia University Press, New York, 1971.

Walker, T. J., **Whale Primer.** Cabrillo Historical Association, San Diego, Calif., 1975.

Winn, H. E., and B. L. Olla, *Behavior of Marine Animals: Current Perspectives in Research.* Volume 3. "Cetaceans." Plenum Press, New York, 1979.

INDEX